Atlas of World History

World Wars and Globalization
1914–2010

BROWN
BEAR
BOOKS

Published by Brown Bear Books Limited

An imprint of:
The Brown Reference Group Ltd
68 Topstone Road
Redding
Connecticut 06896
USA
www.brownreference.com

© 2009 The Brown Reference Group Ltd

ISBN: 978-1-933834-70-2

Editorial Director: Lindsey Lowe
Senior Managing Editor: Tim Cooke
Managing Editor: Rachel Tisdale
Editor: Louise Spilsbury
Designer: Rob Norridge

Library of Congress Cataloging-in-Publication Data available upon request

Picture Credits

Cover Image
Corbis: Regis Bossu/Sygma

Artwork © The Brown Reference Group Ltd

The Brown Reference Group Ltd has made every effort to trace copyright holders of the pictures used in this book. Anyone having claims to ownership not identified above is invited to contact The Brown Reference Group Ltd.

Printed in the United States of America

Contents

Introduction   4

The World in 1920   6

The World in 1950   8

The World in 1974   10

The World in 2005   12

World War I   14

Interwar Europe   18

World War II in Europe to 1942   22

World War II in Europe
    1942–1945   26

Europe Divided   30

Europe after the Cold War   34

The Americas to 1945   38

The Americas Since 1945   42

Central America and the
    Caribbean   46

The Making of the Soviet Union   50

The Decline of the Soviet Union   54

China 1911–1949   58

Japan and Asia   62

World War II in Asia   66

East Asia Since 1945   72

Central and South Asia   78

The Rise of the Pacific Rim   84

The Middle East and North Africa 90

Arab–Israeli Conflict   94

The Middle East Since 1977   98

Decolonization and Nationalism
    in Africa   102

Glossary   106

Further Reading   108

Index   110

Introduction

Atlas of World History forms part of the Curriculum Connections series. The six volumes of this set cover all the major periods of the World History curriculum: The First Civilizations (4,000,000–500 BCE); The Classical World (500 BCE–600 CE); The Middle Ages (600–1492); The Early Modern World (1492–1783); Industrialization and Empire (1783–1914); and World Wars and Globalization (1914–2010).

About this set

Each volume in *Atlas of World History* features thematic world and regional maps. All of the regional maps are followed by an in-depth article.

The volume opens with a series of maps that provide an overview of the world at particular dates. They show at-a-glance how the shape of the world changed during the period covered in the book. The rest of the volume is divided into regional sections, each of which covers a continent or part of a continent. Within each section, maps appear in broadly chronological order. Each map highlights a particular period or topic, which the accompanying article explains in a concise but accurate summary.

Within each article, two key aids to learning are located in sidebars in the margins of each page:

Curriculum Context sidebars indicate that a subject has particular relevance to certain key state and national World and American history guidelines and curricula. They highlight essential information or suggest useful ways for students to consider a subject or to include it in their studies.

Glossary sidebars define key words within the text.

At the end of the book, a summary Glossary lists the key terms defined in the volume. There is also a list of further print and Web-based resources and a full volume index.

About this book

World Wars and Globlization is a fascinating guide to the history of humankind from the outbreak of World War I to the present day.

The volume begins with a series of maps that present an overview of the grand themes of history at key dates between 1914 and the end of the 20th century. The maps chart the shifting pattern of human settlement and the rise and fall of empires and states, in addition to reviewing the spread of trade and migration on a world scale.

The regional maps that follow look more closely at the great events of the period: the World Wars, the rise and fall of communism in Russia and Europe, the aftermath of colonialism in Africa and Asia, and the turmoil of the Middle East. There is also coverage of less familiar histories, such as those of Korea during the period of Japanese rule and the civil war of Liberia.

TYPOGRAPHICAL CONVENTIONS

World maps

FRANCE	state or empire
Belgian Congo	dependency or territory
Mongols	tribe, chiefdom or people
Anasazi culture	cultural group

Regional maps

HUNGARY	state or empire
Bohemia	dependency or territory
Slavs	tribe, chiefdom or people
ANATOLIA	geographical region
✗	battle
•	site or town

The World in 1920

After World War I the League of Nations, led by Britain and France, sought to prevent further global conflicts. However, the isolationism of the United States and the interest of Japan only in China and the Pacific made the League less widespread and effective than hoped for. The new globalizing force of air travel, meanwhile, increasingly linked territories worldwide.

Belgian territory

British empire and dominions

Dutch territory

French territory

Italian territory

Japanese territory

Portuguese territory

Spanish territory

United States territory

League of Nations mandate

ITALY founding member of League of Nations, 1919

✴ theater of World War I

→ pioneer air route

SOVIET RUSSIA

FINLAND

LATVIA

BELORUSSIA

UKRAINE

ROMANIA

BULGARIA

GEORGIA

TURKEY

AZERBAIJAN

ARMENIA

PERSIA

Palestine

Syria

Iraq

Kuwait

Egypt

Qatar

NEJD

HIJAZ

Trucial Oman

Oman

Eritrea

Aden

YE

Sudan

ETHIOPIA

Uganda

Belgian Congo

British East Africa

Rwanda–Urundi

Tanganyika

Nyasaland

Mozambique

Madagascar

Swaziland

Basutoland

SOUTH AFRICA

Autonomous Turkic peoples

AFGHANISTAN

R and K Smith, 1919

MONGOLIA

CHINESE REPUBLIC

FAR EASTERN SSR

Japanese occupation

Sakhalin

Korea

JAPAN

TIBET

NEPAL

BHUTAN

Macao (Portugal)

Taiwan

Hong Kong (Britain)

India

Burma

SIAM

French Indo-China

Philippine Islands

Goa

Ceylon

Sumatra

Malay states

Singapore (Britain)

Borneo

Celebes

Java

Dutch East Indies

Portuguese Timor

New Guinea

North East New Guinea (Australia)

Territory of Papua (Australia)

Mariana Islands

Guam (United States)

(Japan)

Marshall Islands

Palau Islands

Caroline Islands

Solomon Islands (Britain)

Gilbert Islands (Britain)

Ellice Islands (Britain)

New Hebrides (Britain/France)

Fiji Islands (Britain)

New Caledonia (France)

AUSTRALIA

Tasmania

NEW ZEALAND

The World in 1950

In the aftermath of World War II, many newly independent states emerged. The United Nations aimed to unite countries around the world, yet the Cold War divided up the globe into two opposed camps: NATO and the Soviet Union and their respective allies. New socio-economic regional groups formed, including the Arab League and the Organization of American States.

newly independent state,
1942–50

NATO member

Communist country and
administrative area

Organization of American
States member

Arab League founder member

CUBA   United Nations founder member

other state or territory

FINLAND

UNION OF SOVIET SOCIALIST REPUBLICS

ROMANIA

BULGARIA

EGE

TURKEY

LEBANON

SYRIA
SYRIA
rance

ISRAEL

EGYPT

IRAN

IRAQ

JORDAN

Kuwait
(Britain)

Qatar
(Britain)

Bahrain
(Britain)

TO

SAUDI
ARABIA

Oman
(Britain)

Eritrea
(Britain)

YE

Aden
(Britain)

Sudan
(Britain/Egypt)

ETHIOPIA

French
Equatorial

Urundi
Belgium)

Uganda
(Britain)

gian Congo
Belgium)

British Somaliland
(Britain)

French Somaliland
(France)

Italian Somaliland
(Britain)

British East Africa
(Britain)

la
gal)

rn
n)

Tanganyika
(Britain)

SR.

Nyasaland
(Britain)

Mozambique
(Portugal)

Madagascar
(France)

OUTH
FRICA

Swaziland
(Britain)

Basutoland
(Britain)

MONGOLIA

AFGHAN-
ISTAN

PAKISTAN

NEPAL

BHUTAN

PAKISTAN

INDIA

BURMA

PEOPLE'S
REPUBLIC OF
CHINA

NORTH
KOREA

SOUTH
KOREA

JAPAN
(United States occupied)

Sakhalin

Macao
(Portugal)

Hong Kong
(Britain)

TAIWAN
(Nationalist China)

THAILAND

CEYLON

Sumatra

French
Indo-China
(France)

PHILIPPINES

Brunei
(Britain)

Malaya
(Britain)

Singapore
(Britain)

Borneo

Celebes

Mariana Islands
(United States)

Marshall Islands
(United States)

Palau Islands
(United States)

Caroline Islands
(United States)

INDONESIA

Java

New Guinea

Dutch New
Guinea
(Netherlands)

Portuguese
Timor
(Portugal)

Territory of
Papua and
New Guinea
(Australia)

Solomon
Islands
(Britain)

Gilbert
Islands
(Britain)

Ellice Islands
(Britain)

New Hebrides
(Britain/France)

New
Caledonia
(France)

Fiji Islands
(Britain)

AUSTRALIA

Tasmania

NEW
ZEALAND

The World in 1974

By 1974, rising global oil demand and exploration had united many Arab League members, along with others including Nigeria, Venezuela, and Indonesia, into OPEC, an organization controlling oil supply and price. Newly independent states emerged in Africa and Southeast Asia. Cracks in the Warsaw Pact became visible following uprisings against Soviet control in Hungary and Czechoslovakia.

newly independent state, 1950–74

NATO member

Communist country and administrative area

Warsaw Pact member

Arab League member

GABON OPEC member

other state or territory

FINLAND

UNION OF SOVIET SOCIALIST REPUBLICS

ROMANIA

BULGARIA

EECE

TURKEY

CYPRUS

LE.

ISRAEL

SYRIA

IRAQ

JORDAN

EGYPT

BAHRAIN

SAUDI ARABIA

YA.

DY.

OMAN

SUDAN

ETHIOPIA

French Somaliland (France)

SOMALIA

AR.

UGANDA

WANDA

ZAIRE

RUNDI

KENYA

TANZANIA

la

al)

ZAMBIA

MALAWI

Mozambique (Portugal)

MADAGASCAR

Comoros (France)

MAURITIUS

OUTH FRICA

SWAZILAND

LESOTHO

IRAN

AFGHAN ISTAN

KUWAIT

QATAR

PAKISTAN

NEPAL

BHUTAN

BANGLADESH

INDIA

BURMA

MONGOLIA

PEOPLE'S REPUBLIC OF CHINA

NORTH KOREA

SOUTH KOREA

JAPAN

Sakhalin

Macao (Portugal)

Hong Kong (Britain)

TAIWAN

LAOS

SOUTH VIETNAM

CAMBODIA

THAILAND

SRI LANKA

MALDIVES

N.V.

PHILIPPINES

Mariana Islands (United States)

Marshall Islands (United States)

Brunei (Britain)

MALAYSIA

Palau Islands (United States)

Caroline Islands (United States)

VI

Sumatra

Celebes

Borneo

SINGAPORE

Java

INDONESIA

New Guinea

Portuguese Timor (Portugal)

Papua New Guinea (Australia)

Solomon Islands (Britain)

NAURU

Gilbert Islands (Britain)

Ellice Islands (Britain)

New Hebrides (Britain/France)

New Caledonia (France)

FIJI

TONGA

AUSTRALIA

Tasmania

NEW ZEALAND

The World in 2005

The collapse of the Soviet Union in 1991 left few
Communist nations in the world. Countries
bordering Europe and Central Asia that had been
part of the former Soviet Union became independent
from Russia following peaceful and armed revolts.
The last African countries finally emerged from
European control.

A. Albania
AR. Armenia
AU. Austria
AZ. Azerbaijan
B. Belgium
BO. Bosnia–Herzegovina
CAR. Central African Republic
CR. Croatia
C. Czech Republic
D. Denmark
DR. Dominican Republic
GE. Georgia
GER. Germany
H. Hungary
LE. Lebanon
L. Luxembourg
M. Macedonia (Former Yugoslav Republic of)
N. Netherlands

RO. Romania
S. Switzerland
SK. Saint Kitts–Nevis
SV. Saint Vincent & the Grenadines
SL. Slovakia
SLV. Slovenia
SM. Serbia and Montenegro
U. United Arab Emirates

newly independent state
since 1974

NATO member

Communist country and
administrative area

other state or territory

✳ secessionist states
(unrecognised)

RUSSIAN FEDERATION

FINLAND

ESTONIA
LATVIA
LITHUANIA
BELARUS
UKRAINE
MOLDOVA
SI. Dnestr Republic
RO.
BULGARIA
GE. KAZAKHSTAN
Abkhazia
South Ossetia
AR.
UZBEKISTAN
KYRGYZSTAN
TURKMENISTAN
TAJIKISTAN
AZ.
Karabakh
TURKEY
orthern Cyprus
SYRIA
CYPRUS
LE.
ISRAEL
IRAN
AFGHAN-
ISTAN
IRAQ
KUWAIT
JORDAN
EGYPT
QATAR
BAHRAIN
U.
SAUDI
ARABIA
OMAN
YEMEN
NEPAL
PAKISTAN
BANGLADESH
INDIA
MYANMAR
BHUTAN
MONGOLIA

PEOPLE'S
REPUBLIC OF
CHINA

NORTH
KOREA
SOUTH
KOREA
JAPAN
Sakhalin

TAIWAN

LAOS
VIETNAM
THAILAND
CAMBODIA
PHILIPPINES

Northern
Mariana Islands
(United States)

DJIBOUTI
Somaliland
ERITREA
SUDAN
ETHIOPIA
AR.
UGANDA
SOMALIA
SRI
LANKA
MALDIVES
KENYA
RWANDA
DEMOCRATIC
REPUBLIC OF
CONGO
BURUNDI
TANZANIA
SEYCHELLES
COMOROS
OLA
ZAMBIA
MALAWI
E
MOZAMBIQUE
MADAGASCAR
MAURITIUS
SWAZILAND
OUTH
FRICA
LESOTHO

BRUNEI
MALAYSIA
SINGAPORE
Sumatra
Kalimantan
(Borneo)
Sulawesi
Java
INDONESIA
EAST TIMOR
New Guinea
PAPUA
NEW GUINEA

FEDERATED STATES
OF MICRONESIA
PALAU

MARSHALL
ISLANDS

NAURU
KIRIBATI
SOLOMON
ISLANDS
TUVALU

VANUATU
New
Caledonia
(France)
FIJI
TONGA

AUSTRALIA

Tasmania

NEW
ZEALAND

World War I

In 1914 tensions between two hostile alliances—Germany and Austria–Hungary on one side and France, Russia, and Britain on the other—erupted into World War I.

World War I

Before 1914, Europe had enjoyed unprecedented prosperity, the fruits of industrialization, and a century without a general war. Yet two alliances, the Allied powers (the United Kingdom, France, and Russia) and the Central powers (Germany, Austria–Hungary and, later, the Ottoman empire), were preparing for war.

Curriculum Context

It is important to understand the relative importance of economic and political rivalries, ethnic and ideological conflicts, militarism, and imperialism as underlying causes of the war.

The main reason was the ambition and instability of Germany. The country had enjoyed a period of rapid industrialization, replacing Britain as the main motor of Europe's economy, and its industrial strength was matched by its military might. One of Germany's oldest ambitions (one which brought it into conflict with Russia) was to expand eastward. Germany believed it was encircled by hostile powers and was intent on protecting its interests, and those of Austria–Hungary, in southern Europe, the Ottoman empire, and the Middle East.

Fighting on two fronts

In a long war, the strain of fighting on two fronts would inevitably tell. Military planners sought to combat this by launching a knockout blow against France and then transporting troops to the east to face the Russian army. But the plan failed when, in August 1914, war broke out following a crisis over Austrian and Russian influence in the Balkans. The French army was swiftly mobilized and halted the exhausted German army 80 kilometers (50 miles) short of Paris. Stalemate followed on the Western Front; the war was bogged down in trench warfare, as the defensive capabilities of the machine gun dominated the war until new tactics, using tanks and artillery more intelligently, were developed in 1917. Despite early victories against the Russians, the Germans now had to cope with war on two fronts.

Western Front

Line of battle between the Allies and Germany in WWI, which stretched from the English Channel across France and Belgium.

German successes

In the Balkans, victories by the Central powers over Serbia and Romania (and the entry of the Ottomans into the war in 1915) seemed to create the kind of political and trading empire that Germany wanted. In 1917 czarist Russia collapsed, its economy and political system exhausted by the demands of the war. Early in 1918, its revolutionary Bolshevik government withdrew from the war, leaving Germany in control of much of the Ukraine and southern Russia. German colonial ambitions in Europe seemed satisfied at last.

Allied efforts

During 1916 Allied economic power began to assert itself. Britain developed a war economy, supplying munitions and other war materiel manufactured at home or imported from the United States and its empire. The German navy tried to break Allied lines of supply by torpedoing British shipping; but when unrestricted submarine warfare began in 1917, the United States joined the war on the Allied side— though more as a supplier of munitions than as a belligerent. The Allies blockaded German ports, intensifying German economic difficulties.

Victory of the Allies

The years 1916–17 saw several costly battles on the Western Front—notably Verdun, the Somme, and Ypres—made possible by the huge buildup of arms on the Allied side. The Central powers decided to make a tactical withdrawal on the Western Front and to militarize the economy at home. The result was disastrous. By November 1918, the German army had not retreated to within its own borders (it had in fact made large advances the previous spring) but was in clear disarray, while food and fuel shortages led to the country collapsing from within. Kaiser Wilhelm II abdicated, as did the emperor of Austria–Hungary. The Allies were in a position to dictate the terms of peace.

Curriculum Context

Students studying World War I should understand how the Russian Revolution and the entry of the United States affected the course and outcome of the war.

Materiel

Equipment and supplies of a military force.

Curriculum Context

An important aspect of the war is the way massive industrial production and innovations in military technology affected war strategy and tactics, and its scale and duration.

Interwar Europe

During the interwar years Europe was sharply divided over which leaders could solve the economic and social crises facing it: those from the extreme left or the extreme right.

area temporarily independent

— border, 1921

dictatorships by 1 Sep 1939

Communist

fascist

other

1924 date of introduction of dictatorship

democracies, 1939

British territories and mandates

French territories and mandates

other

German gain, 1935–1 Sep 1939

Hungarian gain, 1938–39

Italian gain, Apr 1939

Turkish gain, 1923

Nationalist-held Spain, late 1936

Nationalist gain by Dec 1938

demilitarized zone, 1919–35

area of economic revival

area of economic decline

SPAIN country experiencing civil war, with date

✳ strike, riot or other protest action

✳ Communist uprising, 1919–23

✳ international incident

✳ incident of Polish aggression, 1920

☨ city with large Jewish population

— supply route for Spanish civil war

▷ emigration of more than 200,000 refugees

Trondheim•

Umeå•

FINLAND
independent 1917/20

Lake
Onega

Bergen•

NORWAY

Gävle•

Turku✿

Helsinki

Russians

Lake
Ladoga

✿Leningrad
(Petrograd)

Sundsvall•

Oslo✿
(Christiania)

SWEDEN

Stockholm•

Tallinn
(Revel)✿

ESTONIA
independent 1918
1933

Lake
Peipus

Pskov•

UNION OF SOVIET
SOCIALIST REPUBLICS
1917–21,
1917

•Moscow

Göteborg•

Vänern

Vättern

Baltic Sea

LATVIA
independent 1918
✿**1934**

Riga

Western Dvina

Vitebsk•

✿

•Smolensk

DENMARK

Copenhagen•

✿Memel
1939 to Germany

LITHUANIA
independent 1918
1926

Kaunas•

Vilna•

Belorussia
independent 1919–21

Poles

•Minsk

RLANDS

Cuxhaven•

1933

Schleswig
Lübeck

Königsberg✿
Gdynia✿

East
Prussia
to Germany

Brest-Litovsk

✿Kiev

•Kharkov

Kiel✿
Hamburg✿

•Rostock

Danzig
(free city)
1919

Polish Corridor

The Curzon Line

Russians

RLANDS

1919–23,
1930–33

Bremen•

Stettin✿
1919–23,
1930–33

Germans

Warsaw✿
✿1920

Poles

Amsterdam•
The Hague•

German Jews

Berlin✿

Magdeburg✿

Oder

Lodz
1936

POLAND
1926

Lvov

Dnieper

Ukraine
independent 1917–20

Dnepropetrovsk
(Yekaterinoslav)

1932
Brussels
Lille•1936

GERMANY
Essen **1933**

Leipzig

1938 to
Germany

Breslau•

Vistula

✿Krakow
1936

Teschen
1936

GIUM

uen

Düsseldorf•

Cologne•

Frankfurt•

Sudetenland

Prague•

Bohemia
Moravia

CZECHOSLOVAKIA
1938–39

1939 to
Hungary

Iasi•

Kishinev•

Dniester

SAAR
1919 to
e of Nations,
to Germany

LUXEMBOURG
1939 to Germany

Nuremberg•

Vienna✿

Slovakia

1938 to
Hungary

Hungarians

✡Odessa

Strasbourg•

Bavaria

AUSTRIA
1934

Budapest•

ROMANIA
1938

CE

Munich•
1919–23,
1930–33

1938 to Germany
1938

HUNGARY
1931–35

Timisoara•

Ploiesti•
1934✿

Bucharest•

Black Sea

Berne•

SWITZERLAND

Geneva✿
1932

Lyon•

LIECHTENSTEIN

Locarno✿

Trieste✿

Bergamo•

Venice•

Zagreb•
1935–38

Danube

Varna•

1921–34

Milan•
Turin✿
1919–22

Fiume 1919

Zara
1920 to Italy

Belgrade✿
1935–38

Burgas•

1919–1922 to Greece,
1923 to Turkey

Bologna•
1919–22

SAN
MARINO

Sava

Kragujevac•

BULGARIA
1934

Genoa•

Florence•

KINGDOM OF THE SERBS,
CROATS AND SLOVENES
(Yugoslavia from 1931)
1929

BELGRADE

Sofia•
Plovdiv•

Istanbul•

Ankara•

MONACO

ITALY
1925

Skopje•

Edirne•

Marseille•
1936

1919–22

Corsica
to France

Rome•
1919–22

1937

Tirane•

Thessalonica•

Turks

TURKEY
1924

Chanak
1922✿

Sakarya
River
1921

nia
ent 1932–38
celona

Naples•
1919–22

Sardinia
to Italy

Bari
1919–22

ALBANIA
1939 to Italy

1934

Izmir✿
1922

Greeks

1919–22 to Greece,
1923 to Turkey

1923
Corfu
to Greece

GREECE
1936

Islands
ain

Palermo•

Sicily

Patras•

Athens•
1933, 1935

Rhodes
Dodecanese
1920 to Greece,
1923 to Italy

Cyprus
to Britain

Crete

Tunis•

Malta
to Britain

Mediterranean
Sea

ria
ance

Tunisia
French
protectorate

Tripoli•

Benghazi•

Cyrenaica
to Italy

Alexandria•

EGYPT
1922 independent

•Cairo

Tripolitania
to Italy

Interwar Europe

World War I destroyed the old order in central and eastern Europe: the fall of the Romanovs (Russia), Habsburgs (Austria–Hungary), and Hohenzollerns (Germany) brought political instability on top of the war's economic and social dislocation. Extremism flourished in central Europe, where Marxist revolutions were countered by a rightwing backlash.

Curriculum Context

It is important to understand how the collapse of the German, Hapsburg, and Ottoman empires and the creation of new states affected international relations in Europe and the Middle East.

The peace treaties failed to create a lasting settlement, and provided instead the grounds for future discontent. United States president Wilson hoped that ethnically homogeneous nation-states would eradicate nationalist rivalries and squabbling over territory, but this proved impossible. Two new states (Czechoslovakia and the Kingdom of the Serbs, Croats, and Slovenes—later Yugoslavia) and one reconstituted one (Poland) assembled many ethnic groups within arbitrary borders, and nationalist groups were often disappointed in disputed areas. Italy, its promises from the Allies for territory unfulfilled, set out to take the territory it claimed by force, as did Poland.

Treaty troubles

The Treaty of Versailles forced Germany to admit guilt for starting the war and to pay huge reparations to the Allies. The League of Nations, set up to resolve disputes arising from the settlement, had no power because the United States declined to join. Britain and France were economically weak after the war and sought to keep Germany weak as well. France occupied the Ruhr in 1923 to enforce payment of reparations, but the hyper-inflation that ensued in Germany provided fertile ground for extremist groups. With Germany's prosperity essential for European well-being, reparations were reduced and a limited recovery followed, funded by American loans.

Curriculum Context

Students studying interwar Europe should understand how the League of Nations was founded and assess its promise and limitations as a vehicle for achieving lasting peace.

Depression and dictators

During the depression of the early 1930s, caused in part by the withdrawal of American loans, massive unemployment and protest were followed by a return to authoritarian government. The dictator Pilsudski had upheld Catholicism in Poland since 1926; now Franco did the same in Spain after a three-year civil war (1936–39). This bloody conflict became a war by proxy between the Soviet-supplied republicans and German- and Italian-supported right.

The rise of Fascism

Promising national renewal and fueled by grievances over the peace settlement, Mussolini's Fascist movement in Italy was established as a totalitarian regime in 1925. Fascist parties formed across Europe and in 1933 Hitler's Nazi party won power in Germany, its appeal magnified by mass unemployment—the Nazis eliminated unemployment by means of public work schemes—and fear of Communism.

The road to war

Britain and France tried to buy off the dictators by conceding small territorial claims (the policy of "appeasement"), but the dictators demanded more. Italy escaped virtually unpunished for invading Ethiopia in 1935 as Britain and France attempted to preserve Mussolini as an ally against Germany. Hitler, as well as initiating his anti-Jewish policies, began to challenge the Treaty of Versailles: in 1935 Germany rearmed and in 1936 it reoccupied the Rhineland. German territory was further extended with the Anschluss with Austria (1938) and the partition of Czechoslovakia (agreed with Britain and France at Munich in 1938). Germany invaded Czechoslovakia in 1939 and the French and British guaranteed the security of several other European states, but to little avail. Germany invaded Poland on September 1; Britain and France declared war on Germany on September 3.

Curriculum Context

The effects of United States isolationist policies are an important aspect of world politics and international relations in the 1920s.

Appeasement

Tactic of giving in to the demands of an aggressive nation in an attempt to avoid war.

Curriculum Context

The legacy of World War I, the depression, ethnic and ideological conflicts, imperialism, and traditional political or economic rivalries are underlying causes of World War II.

World War II in Europe to 1942

During the first half of World War II, Hitler's armed forces outmaneuvered and defeated Allied forces to such an extent that Germany dominated Europe.

N

summer route

from Canada and the United States

Reykjavik • ICELAND

Faroe Islands
to Denmark

winter route to Murmansk and Archangel

Shetland Islands
to Britain

Bergen •

Stavanger •

from Canada and the United States

Glasgow •

Newcastle •

North Sea

Belfast • UNITED
IRELAND KINGDOM
Dublin • Liverpool Hull
Manchester • Sheffield
Birmingham • Coventry
Cardiff • Bristol London
Southampton • Dover
Plymouth • Dunkirk
Portsmouth • Dieppe
Le Havre

Bergen-
Belser
B
Westerbork

NETH
Rotter

Brussels
BELGIUM

*ATLANTIC
OCEAN*

Brest • St Malo Paris
Lorient • St Nazaire
FRANCE
Vichy •
La Rochelle Lyon

occupied by
Germany,
Nov 1942
Bayonne • Toulouse

SWITZ

occupied G
by Italy,
Nov 1942

Bordeaux •
Bilbao •

ANDORRA

Toulon

Cors
Vichy con
until Nov 1

Douro
Barcelona •

Nov 1942

SPAIN
Tagus Madrid •

Guadiana
Lisbon • Valencia •

Balearic
Islands
to Spain

Sardin
to It

Seville •

Cádiz •

Gibraltar
to Britain

Algiers •

July 1940

Tangier • to Spain
Spanish Morocco Oran •

Algeria
Vichy control
until Nov 1942

Nov 1942

Nov 1942 Fez •

Fedala •

*French
Morocco*
Vichy control until
Nov 1942

Safi •

Legend

- Germany, 1 Sep 1939
- territory gained by USSR, 1939–40
- western frontier of USSR, June 1941
- area of population and industry evacuated to Siberia, 1941–42
- borders, June 1942
- Axis power, June 1942
- ally of Axis power, June 1942
- under Axis occupation, June 1942
- Vichy territory, June 1942
- under Allied control, June 1942
- furthest Axis advance, 1941
- front lines, end Nov 1942
- Maginot line
- ⬢ bombed city, 1940–42
- ⬤ U-boat base
- ♯ siege
- ⬧ atrocity or mass murder
- Lidice reprisal killing
- ▦ death camp
- ▦ concentration camp
- ⬤ Axis airborne operation
- ⬤ British commando raid
- ➡ Allied withdrawal
- ➡ Axis offensive
- ➡ Allied offensive
- main convoy route, 1941–42

World War II in Europe to 1942

The declaration of war on Germany by Britain and France in 1939 took Hitler by surprise; he was now forced to deal with the threat to Germany's western flank in order to avoid fighting the war on two fronts. His primary objective, though, remained the conquest of the Soviet Union.

Germany and the Soviet Union divided Poland between them as agreed in the 1939 Nazi–Soviet pact, both sides deporting large numbers of people. The USSR later absorbed the Baltic states with the exception of Finland, which retained its independence in the "Winter War" of 1939–40. A "phoney war" ensued, the first break in the inactivity being the German invasion of Denmark and Norway in April 1940.

Phoney war

Period during a war when enemies are not actively engaged in armed conflict.

German advances

Winston Churchill took over as British prime minister in May, but Allied resistance was ineffectual during the German attack on the Low Countries and France in the same month. France surrendered within six weeks. Germany occupied the north, while a collaborationist regime at Vichy controlled the south; Belgium and the Netherlands became satellites in the German industrial complex. Britain evacuated most of its forces from northern France, but the Battle of Britain of 1940 (the first decisive battle fought in the air) stifled plans for a seaborne invasion by denying air superiority to the Luftwaffe (German air force). Italy chose this point to enter the war. The Mediterranean was closed to British shipping and fighting began in north and east Africa.

Curriculum Context

Students studying World War II should compare it to World War I in terms of the impact of industrial production, political goals, national mobilization, and technological innovations.

The Barbarossa campaign

While the air offensive continued against Britain and escalated into the Blitz, Hitler turned his attention to the east. By the summer of 1940 he was planning the Barbarossa campaign—an invasion of the Soviet Union.

In April 1941 German, Bulgarian, and Italian forces invaded Greece and Yugoslavia to secure their southern flank for Barbarossa. Italy had been defeated in Greece the previous year but now the Axis forces overran all opposition, driving British troops first to Crete and then to Egypt. German success had been based on *blitzkrieg* or lightning war. Tanks, dive-bombers, and motorized infantry destroyed defenses before reserves could be mobilized or a war of attrition develop. Barbarossa began on June 22, 1941, and was expected to last six weeks, but by November the advance was bogged down by the weather. Hitler had ignored advice to seize Moscow and advanced on all fronts. His forces were now dangerously stretched.

The Allied counter-offensive

Stalin launched an offensive in the spring of 1942, but the Germans occupied more territory in the summer. It became clear, however, that they could not launch a knockout blow: the vast size of the country and its population, and the safety of the industrial areas evacuated east of the Urals meant that the USSR had huge capacity. The United States had already been supplying Britain and the Soviet Union with materiel through the "lend–lease" scheme, and its entry into the war as a full belligerent in December 1941 gave the Allies a major boost. From then on Allied superiority in men and arms, and Hitler's lack of strategic vision, were to lead to German defeat.

> **War of attrition**
> When a belligerent force attempts to win a war by wearing down its enemy to the point of collapse.

> **Curriculum Context**
> Students studying World War II should focus on the major turning points of the war. The events of 1942 are a good example of this.

Nazi death camps

Hitler hoped to create a "new order" based on ideas of Nazi superiority. Millions of Slavs and Gypsies were shot, deported, starved, or enslaved to create a "living space" for Germans. In the "final solution," mass shootings and gassings were used to exterminate the Jews and others. Death camps were built and, by the end of 1942, almost the entire Jewish population of Poland, the USSR as far east as the Caucasus, and the Baltic states — about three million people—had been killed.

World War II in Europe 1942–1945

The turning point in World War II came in 1942. Hitler suffered severe setbacks and from then on the Allies continued to advance and liberate occupied territories.

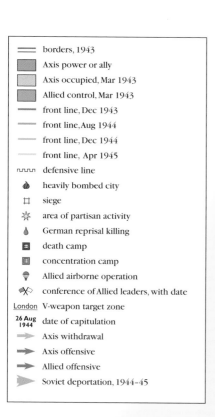

Key:
- borders, 1943
- Axis power or ally
- Axis occupied, Mar 1943
- Allied control, Mar 1943
- front line, Dec 1943
- front line, Aug 1944
- front line, Dec 1944
- front line, Apr 1945
- defensive line
- heavily bombed city
- siege
- area of partisan activity
- German reprisal killing
- death camp
- concentration camp
- Allied airborne operation
- conference of Allied leaders, with date
- London   V-weapon target zone
- 26 Aug 1944   date of capitulation
- Axis withdrawal
- Axis offensive
- Allied offensive
- Soviet deportation, 1944–45

Reykjavik   ICELAND

Tror

Faroe Islands to Denmark

Shetland Islands to Britain

Bergen

North Sea

Glasgow   Edinburgh
Belfast   Newcastle
IRELAND   UNITED KINGDOM
Dublin   Liverpool   Manchester   Wilhelmshaven
Birmingham   Lincoln   Hanove
Cambridge   Coventry   Arnhem Sep 1944
Oxford   London   Bochu
Southampton   Reading   July 1942   Düsseldorf   Essen
Plymouth   Lille   BELGIUM   Cologne
June 1944   Portsmouth   Le Havre   Sep 1944   Frankfurt
NORMANDY   Caen   Trier   Nuren
Brest   Falaise   July 1944   Siegfried Line
Aug 1944   Le Mans   Paris   Mulhausen
ATLANTIC OCEAN
Nantes   Loire   Jura   Berne
Aug 1944   SWITZERLA
Oradour-sur-Glane   Lyon
Bordeaux   Turin   May
FRANCE   Nice   Genoa
liberated by Sep 1944   Fl
Bilbao   Toulouse   Marseille
ANDORRA
Douro   Corsica to France
SPAIN   Barcelona
Madrid
PORTUGAL   Tagus   Balearic Islands to Spain   Sardinia to Italy
Lisbon   Guadiana   Valencia
Seville   Algiers   Tur
Cádiz   Jan–Feb 1943
Tangier   Gibraltar to Britain   Oran   Tunisia liberated b
Spanish Morocco to Spain   Algeria   May 1943
Free French   Feb 1943
Fez   Mareth Line
Casablanca   French
Jan 1943   Morocco
Free French

Ebro

Murmansk

Narvik

Umeå

Sundsvall

SWEDEN
Gävle
Vänern
Göteborg
Vättern
Stockholm

Copenhagen

Rostock
Peenemünde
Königsberg
Feb–May 1945

FINLAND
4 Sep 1944

Turku
Helsinki
Tallinn

Lake Onega

Lake Ladoga

Leningrad
1941–44

Pskov

Baltic Sea

Memel
Danzig

Riga

Lake Peipus

Vitebsk

Minsk

Reichskommissariat
Ostland
liberated by 1945

Archangel

Kotlas

Demyansk

Smolensk

UNION OF SOVIET
SOCIALIST REPUBLICS

Moscow
Oct 1943

Gorki

Crimean Tatars

Germans and Poles

Berlin
Apr–May 1945

Bialystok

Warsaw

GERMANY
8 May 1945

Leipzig
Breslau
Dresden
Prague
Auschwitz

Regensburg
Munich
Vienna

INNSBRUCK
Dec 1944–Mar 1945

Trieste
Zagreb

Venice
Zara

Bologna

ITALY
Sep 1943

Rome

General
Government
of Poland

Krakow

Lvov

Reichskommissariat
Ukraine
liberated by spring 1944

June 1944

June–July 1944

July 1944

June 1944

SLOVAKIA

Bratislava

HUNGARY
31 Dec 1944

Budapest
Sep–Dec 1945

Transylvania

Banat

Iasi

Kishinev

Transnistria

Kiev

Orel

Kursk
June–Aug
1943

Kharkov
Feb–Mar
1943

Dnieper

Dnepropetrovsk

Rostov

Bulgarians &
Romanians

Sep 1943

Sep–Nov 1943

Stalingrad
Sep 1942–Feb 1943

Kalmyks

Caspian Sea

Karachais
Meskhetians
Chechens
Grozny

CAUCASUS MTS.

Baku

Tbilisi

Yerevan

Protectorate of
Bohemia-Moravia

ROMANIA
26 Aug 1944

Ploiesti

Bucharest

Belgrade

Danube

Odessa

Sevastopol
Apr–May 1944

Yalta
Feb 1945

May 1944

Black Sea

Trabzon

CROATIA
Gothic
Line

Sarajevo

YUGOSLAVIA

SERBIA

Split

MONTENEGRO

Gustav Line

Cassino
Jan–Mar 1944

Tirane

ALBANIA
liberated by
Nov 1944

BULGARIA
28 Oct 1944

Varna
Burgas

Sofia
Plovdiv

Skopje

Edirne

Istanbul

Ankara

TURKEY

Adana

Mosul

IRAN

Tehran
Nov 1943

Naples
Salerno

GREECE
liberated by
Oct 1944

Patras

Athens

Izmir

*Rhodes
Dodecanese
to Italy*

*Cyprus
to Britain*

Syria
Free French

Baghdad

IRAQ

Palermo
Sicily

Sep 1943
*Malta
to Britain*

*Mediterranean
Sea*

Crete
Heraklion

Oct 1944

Beirut
Lebanon
Free French

Damascus

Transjordan
to Britain

Palestine
to Britain

Amman

Kuwait
British protectorate

Jerusalem

Tripoli

Benghazi

LIBYA
British protectorate

Alexandria

EGYPT

Cairo
Nov–Dec 1943

World War II in Europe 1942–45

Although 1942 brought a change in fortunes for the Allies, two more years of fighting were needed before the war in Europe was won. The German surrender at Stalingrad was a major blow to Hitler. In July the Soviet army repulsed the Germans at Kursk in the war's biggest land battle; the Red Army then drove west, its next victory being at Kharkov.

In May, the Germans capitulated in north Africa. By mid-1943 Germany had also lost the crucial Battle of the Atlantic, where the Allied use of long-range aircraft made Germany's submarine assault on transatlantic convoy routes less effective. The German war effort intensified with the announcement of total war. The Allies invaded Sicily, Mussolini was deposed, and the Italians sued for peace; however Germany immediately occupied north and central Italy. The Allies' Italian campaign dragged on until the end of the war.

Allied achievements

Allied bombing increased in strength and effectiveness as the Americans joined the British in attacking German cities: the first 1,000-bomber raid took place against Cologne in 1943. The bombing campaign pulled German resources from other fronts and weakened the war economy. In June 1944, the Allies landed in Normandy and liberated France and Belgium. In east and southeast Europe the Red Army defeated both Romania and Bulgaria. Germany pulled out of Greece, but Hungary was kept in the war by a Nazi coup after initially surrendering to the Soviet Union.

Russian involvement

Political as well as military considerations had held back U.S. president Roosevelt from supporting British prime minister Churchill's plan to invade southeast Europe. Unlike Roosevelt, Churchill had little faith in

Total war

The complete mobilization of a country's resources and economy towards its war efforts.

Curriculum Context

Students studying World War II should think about how the political and diplomatic leadership of such individuals as Churchill and Roosevelt affected its outcome.

Stalin's postwar intentions, and Soviet action in Poland did not engender confidence. As the Red Army advanced toward Warsaw, there was a full-scale rising against the German forces in the city. Stalin did not assist the rebels, and when the Germans quashed the revolt 250,000 Poles were killed.

The end of the war

Hitler tried to stop the Allied bomber assault on Germany by firing rocket-powered V-bombs at Britain, but the forces ranged against him were too great. The last German offensive, through the Ardennes at the end of 1944, was a failure and after Hitler's suicide, Germany surrendered on May 8, 1945.

Death and destruction

When Allied troops liberated the Nazi death camps, six million Jews had been killed, along with millions of other nationalities including Ukrainians, Poles, Balts, Belorussians, Russians, and Gypsies. As the Red Army advanced, it took its revenge. Ten million ethnic Germans were expelled from central and eastern Europe; perhaps two million died. The USSR deported five million for alleged collaboration; returning prisoners-of-war often faced exile or death. By 1945 much of Europe was destroyed, its people dead or homeless.

Divisions within Allied forces

Across Europe guerrilla partisan forces fought the Axis powers. Many were divided on ethnic or political lines, and their activities provoked bloody reprisals. A revolt in Slovakia was brutally put down, but in Yugoslavia the Communist-dominated partisans formed the basis of Tito's postwar government; in Prague, a popular rising helped the Soviet advance on the city. In Greece, the Communists defied the British who sought to reestablish the monarchy after the Germans withdrew in October 1944; the resulting civil war ended only with the collapse of the Communists in 1949. Resistance in Poland and countries incorporated into the Soviet Union also continued after the war, but it was now directed against the USSR.

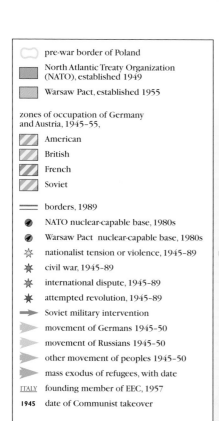

Europe Divided

Europe lived in the shadow of the two superpowers—the Soviet Union and the United States—for decades after World War II and was divided by their opposing political ideologies.

pre-war border of Poland

North Atlantic Treaty Organization (NATO), established 1949

Warsaw Pact, established 1955

zones of occupation of Germany and Austria, 1945–55,

American

British

French

Soviet

borders, 1989

NATO nuclear-capable base, 1980s

Warsaw Pact nuclear-capable base, 1980s

nationalist tension or violence, 1945–89

civil war, 1945–89

international dispute, 1945–89

attempted revolution, 1945–89

Soviet military intervention

movement of Germans 1945–50

movement of Russians 1945–50

other movement of peoples 1945–50

mass exodus of refugees, with date

ITALY founding member of EEC, 1957

1945 date of Communist takeover

ORWAY

SWEDEN

Oslo

Vänern

Göteborg

DENMARK
73 EEC member
hus
Copenhagen • Malmo
nse

GERMAN
DEMOCRATIC
REPUBLIC 1949
Berlin
June 1953
June 1953
Leipzig
Dresden
Bernsdorf
Milovice
Aug 1968
Prague
Nuremberg
Temelin
Brno
Neu Ulm
Munich
Salzburg
Linz
Vienna
AUSTRIA
LIECHTENSTEIN
Graz
Germans
1954
Venice
Trieste
Bologna

ITALY

Rome
Gaeta
Naples
Bari

Palermo
Sicily
Catania
Comiso

Valletta
MALTA
1964 independent

Pori • Tampere
FINLAND
Gävle
Vasteras • Uppsala
Stockholm
Estonians
Linköping
Vättern

Turku
Helsinki
Tapa
Tallinn
Kopu
Estonia

Finns
Leningrad

Riga • Latvia
Liepaja
Latvians
Lithuanians
Kaliningrad
(Königsberg)
to Russia
Lithuanians

Gdansk
(Danzig)
Szczecin
Poznan
Warsaw
Lodz
POLAND 1947
1944-47
Krakow
Lublin
Poles
Vilna
Minsk
Belorussia

Moscow

Vitebsk • Smolensk

Russia

UNION OF SOVIET
SOCIALIST REPUBLICS

Belorussians

Derazhnaya
Ukrainians
Kiev

Lvov

Dnepropetrovsk

CZECHOSLOVAKIA 1948
Aug 1968
Bratislava
Debrecen
Oct-Nov 1956
Budapest
HUNGARY 1947
1955 temporarily
leaves Warsaw Pact
Nov 1956
Magyars
Iasi

Moldavia
Kishinev

Pervomaysk

Zagreb
Sava
Timisoara
ROMANIA 1945
Brasov
Ploiesti
Bucharest

Odessa

Sevastopol

YUGOSLAVIA 1945
Belgrade
Sarajevo
Split
Dubrovnik
Skopje

Albanians,
since 1968
Sofia
BULGARIA 1945
Plovdiv

Turks • Varna
Burgas

Black
Sea

Tiranë
ALBANIA 1945
1968 leaves
Warsaw Pact
GREECE
1952-74, 1982
NATO member,
1981 EEC member
1944-1949

Thessalonica

Edirne • Istanbul

Bursa

TURKEY
1952 NATO member

Izmir

Patras
Athens
since 1974

Konya
Adana

Gaziantep

Aleppo

Heraklion
Crete

Dodecanese
1947 to Greece

Greeks & Turks
Nicosia
1974 1955-77
CYPRUS
1960 independent,
Northern Cyprus occupied by
Turks since 1974

TURKISH REPUBLIC OF
NORTHERN CYPRUS
since 1983

Homs

Beirut
LEBANON
1958
ISRAEL
1948 independent

SYRIA

Damascus

Euphrates

Mediterranean Sea

Europe Divided

The wartime cooperation of the Allies quickly broke down and two blocs emerged: the western democratic countries, which were oriented toward the United States, and the eastern Communist countries dominated by the Soviet Union. The period of tension, competition, and hostility that ensued became known as the "Cold War."

Iron curtain

Political, military, and ideological barrier erected by the Soviet Union to divide itself and Soviet bloc countries of Eastern Europe from the West and other noncommunist areas.

An "iron curtain" was drawn across Europe. Set against the Soviet Union's new influence in eastern Europe, there was a real fear that the rest of the continent would succumb to Communism. With Europe devastated and trying to cope with millions of refugees, the United States produced a massive cash injection ("Marshall Aid") in 1947, becoming the counterweight to Soviet power in the east.

Deepening the divide

In 1948 the Soviets blockaded western-occupied West Berlin and in 1949 the republics of West and East Germany were formally constituted. The same year the North Atlantic Treaty was signed, binding the western nations and the United States in an anti-Soviet alliance (NATO), and Comecon was formed to incorporate the east European countries in a system of Soviet-dominated interstate economic planning. In 1950 U.S. troops returned to Europe as part of NATO after the outbreak of war in Korea (1950–53); the Soviet-led Warsaw Pact (a military alliance of eight European Communist nations) was founded five years later.

Curriculum Context

Students studying Europe after World War II should understand how Western European countries achieved rapid economic recovery.

The economies of East and West

The western countries soon recovered their prosperity, creating economic areas to increase trade. The Benelux Customs Union of 1948 was followed by the creation of the European Coal and Steel Community (ECSC), which laid the basis for the European Economic Community

(EEC) in 1958, later becoming the European Community (EC). Eastern European countries did not enjoy the "economic miracle" seen in West Germany, and felt their national identities to be compromised by Soviet interference. Yugoslavia and Albania preserved their traditions of independent Communism as, to a lesser extent, did Romania. Hungary (1956) and Czechoslovakia (1968) tried more radical escapes from the Soviet bloc but were brought into line by force.

Internal protests

Following the Helsinki agreement of 1975, under which the borders of the German Democratic Republic (East Germany) were recognized and the governments of eastern Europe accepted the principle of observing human rights, dissident activity grew more intense. In 1980 the Polish trade union Solidarity was set up and longstanding popular resentment was manifested in widespread industrial disputes. Protest in western Europe was directed both against the United States (over the Vietnam war or the presence of U.S.-controlled nuclear missiles) or against individual governments. The Paris riots of 1968 were part of a general revolt of youth against authority, as was the Baader–Meinhof terrorist group in West Germany.

The changing face of Europe

In the 1970s, the economic downturn caused by inflation, high public spending, and a rise in oil prices led to unemployment and industrial militancy. British prime minster Margaret Thatcher's introduction of free-market economics and revision of labor legislation brought a year-long miners' strike (1984–85). In the late 1980s the new Soviet leader, Mikhail Gorbachev, slackened the ties binding eastern Europe in an effort to free up the east's economy. Revolutions ensued, first in Poland and then East Germany, Hungary, Bulgaria, Czechoslovakia, and Romania. The old order crumbled and Europe began to take a new shape.

Curriculum Context

Students should focus on the causes and consequences of major Cold War crises, such as the Berlin blockade, the Korean War, and the Polish workers' protest.

Free-market economics

Economic system in which goods and services are bought and sold by individuals or firms without government restrictions.

Europe after the Cold War

The collapse of Soviet power signaled the end of bipolar Europe, but more problems arose: eastern governments faced conflicts and western Europe struggled to develop a true political union.

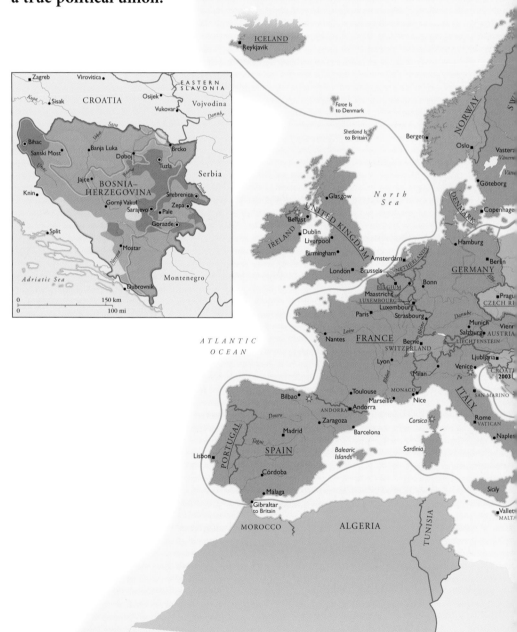

borders, 2005

member state of EU, 2003

state which joined EU in 2004

associated state of EU

state with EU cooperation agreement

member state of EFTA

SPAIN   member state of NATO

1995   year of application for EU membership

former boundary of Warsaw Pact

states which are part of the "open frontier" Schengen agreement

area of ethnic/nationalist tension

territory which has effectively seceded

ethnic composition of Bosnia–Herzegovina, pre-1991

more than 60 percent Croat

more than 60 percent Muslim

more than 60 percent Serb

ethnically mixed area

Bosnian–Croat Federation, 1995

Bosnian Serb Republic, 1995

UN-designated "safe havens"

Oulu

FINLAND

Pori

Lake Onega

Lake Ladoga

Turku

Helsinki

St Petersburg

ckholm

Tallinn

ESTONIA
NATO member from 2004

Lake Peipus

Rybinsk Reservoir

Volga

Riga

LATVIA
NATO member from 2004

Moscow

c

LITHUANIA
NATO member from 2004

Western Drina

grad

Vilna (Vilnius)

Minsk

ian on

BELARUS

KAZAKHSTAN

ND   Warsaw

nber

79

NATO member from 1999

Krakow

Lvov

UKRAINE

Kiev

Kharkov

Dnieper

Aral Sea

OVAKIA

NATO member from 2004

Dnepropetrovsk

Donetsk

Volga

UZBEKISTAN

ara

Budapest

NATO member from 1999

Dniestr Republic

RUSSIAN FEDERATION

GARY

NIA

member from 2004

ROMANIA
NATO member from 2004
1995

Chisinau (Kishinev)

Odessa

Caspian Sea

TURKMENISTAN

Timisoara

Belgrade

Bucharest

Danube

Constanta

Black Sea

Grozny (Dzhokhar Ghala)

Abkhazia

South Ossetia

GEORGIA

Tbilisi

ajevo

SERBIA

BULGARIA
Sofia NATO member from 2004

Varna

Pristina

MONTENEGRO

Plovdiv   **1995**

AZERBAIJAN

Baku

Yerevan

ARMENIA

Karabakh

ane

Skopje

ALBANIA

MACEDONIA
(FORMER YUGOSLAV REPUBLIC OF)

Istanbul

Ankara

Lake Van

Lake Urmia

GREECE

Izmir

TURKEY
1987

IRAN

Patras

Athens

Adana

Gaziantep

terranean Sea

Crete

Nicosia

CYPRUS

LEBANON

SYRIA

IRAQ

Europe after the Cold War

When Communist control over eastern Europe collapsed in 1989, tension between NATO and the Warsaw Pact dissolved. However, many former Soviet satellite countries and, from 1991, the old Soviet republics suffered problems of social restructuring, while western countries faced disagreements over how to cooperate politically and economically.

Exchange Rate Mechanism

System for aligning the exchange rates (how much one currency is worth in terms of the other) of EU currencies against each other, to limit fluctuations in currency exchange.

The price of the reunification of Germany (1990) was high. The former West Germany was faced with a huge bill for taking over East Germany's backward economy. Germany's dominance in European finance meant that the costs of reunion were felt beyond its own borders. Interest rates rose across Europe, and in 1992 Britain and others were forced to leave the Exchange Rate Mechanism (ERM), which had been introduced to guarantee economic stability in the European Union (EU; formerly EC) and lead to eventual monetary union.

Debates within the EU

The failure to maintain the integrity of the ERM called into question the creation of more unified financial structures within the EU. Doubts resurfaced in several member-states about the need for, and price of, a single European currency, planned for introduction in the late 1990s. Parallel with this debate was the question of "widening" the union to include countries that had formerly chosen or been forced to stay outside. While many of the formerly Soviet-dominated countries clamored to join the Union, some countries (including Britain and Denmark) saw fierce anti-EU campaigns, and a referendum on joining led to a "no" vote in Norway. As fears rose of migration, international terrorism, and drug smuggling, doubts arose of the wisdom of the agreement to allow free movement of goods, people, and services across the EU from 1992.

Curriculum Context

Students studying the growth of the European Union should focus on its effects on economic productivity and political integration in Europe.

Instability in the East

The new governments of eastern Europe and the states of the former Soviet Union faced real difficulties in turning state-run command economies into market-driven ones. The nascent democracies often appeared fragile, including Russia, where president Boris Yeltsin faced powerful forces of reaction and radical reform and problems of high unemployment and inflation, potent organized crime, alarming ethnic conflict, and resurgent Russian nationalism.

War in Europe

Meanwhile, resurgent nationalism led to ethnic conflicts in Armenia, Azerbaijan, and Yugoslavia in the 1990s. Here, as elsewhere, different nationalities had been held together by authoritarian Communism. Yugoslavia split into its constituent republics but—unlike in Czechoslovakia where a similar divorce occurred—this took no account of ethnic complexities.

A new era

The war in the former Yugoslavia revealed the impotence of the rest of Europe, which was unable to agree a common policy on the problem, leaving the task of peacekeeping to the United Nations. In 1995, the United States succeeded where Europe had failed, and brokered a settlement in Bosnia. And in 1997 NATO and Russia signed an agreement that allowed for NATO's expansion and ended what remained of the Cold War.

Command economies

Economic systems in which governments make major decisions regarding the production and distribution of goods and services.

Curriculum Context

An important aspect of the changing configuration of political boundaries in the world is the connection between nationalist ideology and the proliferation of sovereign states.

War in Yugoslavia

With the Serbs in the grip of a militant nationalist spirit, and with Bosnia's population divided culturally and religiously between Bosnians, Croats, and Serbs, the conflict focused on Bosnia–Herzogovina and its capital Sarajevo. The states of the former Yugoslavia—especially Bosnia and Croatia—experienced four years of bloody civil war, where atrocities and policies of "ethnic cleansing" forced hundreds of thousands of civilians to flee their homes.

The Americas to 1945

Between 1900 and 1945 the United States rose to international leadership; Latin America underwent transformations in its economic, social, and political spheres.

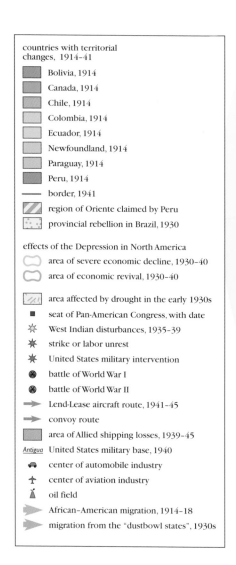

countries with territorial changes, 1914–41

- Bolivia, 1914
- Canada, 1914
- Chile, 1914
- Colombia, 1914
- Ecuador, 1914
- Newfoundland, 1914
- Paraguay, 1914
- Peru, 1914
- —— border, 1941
- region of Oriente claimed by Peru
- provincial rebellion in Brazil, 1930

effects of the Depression in North America

- area of severe economic decline, 1930–40
- area of economic revival, 1930–40
- area affected by drought in the early 1930s
- ■ seat of Pan-American Congress, with date
- ✳ West Indian disturbances, 1935–39
- ✳ strike or labor unrest
- ✳ United States military intervention
- ⊗ battle of World War I
- ⊗ battle of World War II
- ➔ Lend-Lease aircraft route, 1941–45
- ➔ convoy route
- area of Allied shipping losses, 1939–45
- *Antigua* United States military base, 1940
- center of automobile industry
- ✝ center of aviation industry
- ⵊ oil field
- ➤ African–American migration, 1914–18
- ➤ migration from the "dustbowl states", 1930s

The Americas to 1945

World War I (1914–18) involved many of the American nations, despite an original intention to stay out of the conflict. The Caribbean islands and Canada owed direct allegiance to Britain, but most other countries had divided loyalties and were anxious to preserve their own interests; U.S. president Woodrow Wilson advised neutrality.

By 1918 Brazil and several Central American states had joined the Allies; the United States itself stayed out until German U-boat attacks drove Wilson to declare war in 1917. The nation was put on a war footing: the government took over the railroads and strikers were threatened with the draft. Factories and shipyards converted to war work, and thousands of African–Americans moved north to the munitions factories.

The 1920s

By the end of the war, there was little enthusiasm for any U.S. involvement in Europe's postwar territorial arrangements. The Treaty of Versailles and the League of Nations, Wilson's brainchild, were both rejected by Congress as Americans sought "normalcy." The "jazz age" of the 1920s saw a quest for consumer goods and material comfort, despite a moral backlash in the form of the Volstead Act and Prohibition in 1920. The result was a rise in political corruption and gangsterism.

The Great Depression

In 1929, the Wall Street stock market crash heralded the Great Depression, which had global resonance as U.S. loans and investments had propped up world trade. In the United States, the crisis was exacerbated by drought and storms that devastated parts of Texas and the Mid-West. Some 12 million Americans lost their jobs, and shanty-towns (Hoovervilles) sprang up around the main cities. In 1933, president Franklin

---

Prohibition

Period (1919–33) during which the manufacture, import, export, transportation, and sale of intoxicating liquor was banned across the United States.

Curriculum Context

Students studying the Great Depression should focus on its financial, economic, and social causes and on why it spread to most parts of the world.

D. Roosevelt's "New Deal" used government spending to give work to millions on infrastructure projects such as dams and airports. However, agriculture and heavy industry recovered only after 1940, mainly due to U.S. contributions to Britain's war effort. In Canada new political groupings suggested nationalization and the redistribution of income as solutions, while separatists won followers in Quebec. The rise in world prices after 1937 and closer ties with the United States put both proposals on hold for years.

Central and South America

The United States claimed the Caribbean and Central America as its "backyard," intervening to maintain its investments (including the Panama Canal and the oil reserves of Mexico and Venezuela) and building a military base at Guantanamo Bay on Cuba. The region was badly hit by the recession, and several countries turned to dictatorships: some, such as Lázaro Cárdenas, ruler of Mexico from 1934–40, tried honestly to improve the condition of their people. In South America, Colombia and Brazil tried to reduce their economic dependence on the fragile coffee trade in the 1930s by industrial diversification and import substitution. Argentina, which had flourished on grain and meat exports, now had to endure austerity measures. Chile also suffered with the fall in copper prices, while its nitrate exports were hit by the discovery of new chemical methods of production.

World War II

World War II brought full employment and high wages to North America and millions moved to the cities. Convoys took troops and supplies to all main theaters of war, and aid to Britain and the USSR. For the Latin American countries the war years were eased by Roosevelt's "Good Neighbor" Policy. The Coffee Accords of 1940 guaranteed U.S. markets; in return Roosevelt gained bases and promises of military support.

Curriculum Context

Important aspects of the challenges to democratic government in Latin America were economic dependency and United States intervention.

Good Neighbor Policy

Declared intention that the United States would no longer intervene in Latin America to protect private U.S. property interests.

The Americas Since 1945

After World War II the majority of the United States enjoyed an economic boom, while many countries in Latin America struggled with political and environmental problems.

ARCTIC OCEAN

NORTH PACIFIC OCEAN

from Asia

from Asia

Alaska to United States 1959 granted statehood

Gulf of Alaska

Yukon

Great Bear Lake

Great Slave Lake

CA

Lake Winnip

Edmonton

Calgary

Minot

Winni

Gran

Vancouver

Seattle

Minneapolis

Malmstrom

Portland

Ellsworth

Salt Lake City

Denver

Kansas City

Mc

L

R

Sacramento

San Francisco

San José

Los Alamos

Las Vegas

Oklahe City

D.

Los Angeles

Riverside

San Diego

Tijuana

Mexicali

Phoenix

Tucson

Davis-Montham

Ciudad Juarez

El Paso

Aus

San

Chihuahua

Torreón

MEXICO

1992 joins NAFTA

León

Guadalajara

Me City

Tolu

Aca

Farall

UNITED STATES

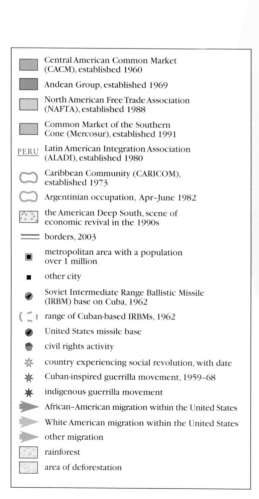

Central American Common Market (CACM), established 1960

Andean Group, established 1969

North American Free Trade Association (NAFTA), established 1988

Common Market of the Southern Cone (Mercosur), established 1991

PERU   Latin American Integration Association (ALADI), established 1980

Caribbean Community (CARICOM), established 1973

Argentinian occupation, Apr–June 1982

the American Deep South, scene of economic revival in the 1990s

borders, 2003

■   metropolitan area with a population over 1 million

■   other city

⊘   Soviet Intermediate Range Ballistic Missile (IRBM) base on Cuba, 1962

(⊏)   range of Cuban-based IRBMs, 1962

◔   United States missile base

✊   civil rights activity

✳   country experiencing social revolution, with date

✳   Cuban-inspired guerrilla movement, 1959–68

✳   indigenous guerrilla movement

➤   African–American migration within the United States

➤   White American migration within the United States

➤   other migration

rainforest

area of deforestation

Labrador Sea

Newfoundland
and Labrador
1949 to Canada

*NORTH
ATLANTIC
OCEAN*

Goose

Gander

Newfoundland

Québec

St Pierre &
Miquelon
to France

Québec

Montréal
Ottawa

*Lake
Ontario*

Boston
Providence
Hartford
New York
Philadelphia
Baltimore
Washington
Norfolk
Richmond

*Lake
Superior*

*Lake
Huron*

*Lake
Erie*

Toronto

Rochester
Buffalo

Detroit

Cleveland
Pittsburgh

Dayton
Columbus
Cincinnati

apolis

Louisville

Greensboro

St Louis

man

Nashville

Charlotte

Memphis
Birmingham
Selma
Montgomery

Atlanta

*Bermuda
to Britain*

Jacksonville

New
Orleans

Orlando
Tampa

Cape Canaveral
(Cape Kennedy)

BAHAMAS

Miami

Potosí

*Gulf of
Mexico*

Havana
Guanajay

Remedios

CUBA
1959

Candelaria

Mérida

*Puerto Rico
to United
States*

St KITTS
& NEVIS

San Juan

ANTIGUA &
BARBUDA

DOMINICA

Port-au-
Prince

Santo Domingo

*DOMINICAN
REPUBLIC*

ST LUCIA

BARBADOS

Kingston

JAMAICA

HAITI

ST VINCENT

GRENADA

TRINIDAD
& TOBAGO

Caribbean Sea

atista

*BELIZE
(British Honduras)*

EMALA

542

HONDURAS

Caracas

Maracay

Maracaibo

Barquisimeto

NICARAGUA
1979–90

Barranquilla

Guatemala
City

Tegucigalpa

San Salvador

Cartagena

VENEZUELA

Georgetown

Paramaribo

*French Guiana
to France*

LVADOR
National
on Front

Managua

Panama
City

San José

COSTA RICA

PANAMA

Medellín

Bogotá

*SURINAME
(Dutch Guiana)*

*GUYANA
(British Guiana)*

Belém

São Luís

Fortaleza

Natal

Recife

COLOMBIA

Cali

Manaus

Maceió

Quito

ECUADOR

Guayaquil

*Amazon
Basin*

Amazon

BRAZIL

Salvador

São Francisco

*Brazilian
Highlands*

Trujillo

Tupac
Amaru

Lima

PERU

Sendero
Luminoso

Arequipa

BOLIVIA

1952–64

La Paz

Santa Cruz

Goiânia

Brasília

*Mato
Grosso
Plateau*

Vitória

Belo Horizonte

Rio de Janeiro

Campinas

São Paulo

Santos

Curitiba

PARAGUAY

Asunción

Itaipú Dam

*SOUTH
ATLANTIC
OCEAN*

to United States and Europe

Porto Alegre

*SOUTH
PACIFIC
OCEAN*

CHILE
left the Andean
Group in 1977

1970–73

Santiago

Valparaíso

Tucumán

Córdoba

Rosario

Mendoza

ARGENTINA

Montoneros

URUGUAY

Tupamaros

Montevideo

La Plata

Buenos Aires

to United States and Europe

Patagonia

South Georgia
to Britain

Stanley

*Falkland Islands
(Islas Malvinas)
to Britain*

The Americas Since 1945

The United States was the undoubted victor of World War II. It suffered only sporadic attacks on its territory and its economy was stimulated by the war. With its unique access to the atomic bomb, the United States looked forward to dominating the postwar world and to realizing its domestic dream of prosperity at home.

U.S. families formed the largest property-owning democracy in the world; they moved in large numbers into aerospace, information technology, automobile, and service industries. Their ambitions led to continuous resettlement within the United States, a pattern imitated by immigrants including Hispanics, Filipinos, and east Asians. Prosperity grew faster than in any other industrialized country, yet the United States failed to abolish the poverty that affected a fifth of the population, to improve healthcare, or to provide real educational opportunity for all. Poverty, especially among black Americans, was a major issue in the Civil Rights campaigns of the 1960s and resurfaced in the 1980s and 1990s.

Impacts of the Cold War

With the start of the Cold War in the late 1940s, a nuclear arms race ensued that developed into the space race of the 1960s. Meanwhile, the United States was drawn into costly conflicts across the globe. The Cold War affected Americans at home, too, with the McCarthy "witchhunts" from 1950. In Cuba, a virtual U.S. client since 1898 but overtaken by socialist–nationalist revolution in 1959, Soviet support for the new Castro regime led to a crisis in 1962. The Soviet Union threatened to use Cuba as a base for nuclear missiles. U.S. dominance was reasserted, but drew criticism for its heavy-handed involvement in the affairs of others.

South American governments

In Chile in 1973, an elected Marxist government was replaced, with U.S. connivance, by a rightwing dictatorship, whose brutal military suppression of opposition was followed in many countries. In the 1940s the charismatic Peróns were popular in Argentina until unemployment, strikes, and inflation destroyed their appeal and brought the army to power. Argentina's military regime sought to revive its flagging popular appeal by invading the British Falkland Islands in 1982. Failure resulted in the civilian government of Carlos Menem, who sought to reduce inflation, privatize industry, and introduce healthcare for workers.

Social and environmental problems

Vested interests of the well-off, combined with policies of international banks to whom most countries were in debt, argued against drastic social change. As a result environmental and social problems associated with a rapidly expanding population worsened (São Paulo and Rio de Janiero were among the world's largest, fastest-growing cities). Indigenous peoples, like the rain forests they inhabited, were treated as expendable in the face of land hunger and mineral-prospecting. Several countries, including Peru, endured violent revolutionary conflicts; in others, such as Colombia, economies were dominated by illegal drug trafficking.

Economic organizations

Many countries entered into economic organizations: Venezuela and Ecuador were founder members of the Organization of Petroleum Exporting Countries (OPEC) in 1960; the Mercosur or Southern Cone Common Market (1991), Latin American Integration Association (1980), and Andean Pact (1969) were attempts at economic cooperation. In 1992, to the dismay of many in the United States and Canada who feared the competition of Third World wages, the North American Free Trade Agreement was extended to include those two countries and Mexico.

Central America and the Caribbean

After the Cuban revolution there was a
wave of regime change and independence
movements through Central America and
the Caribbean.

N

Torréon *Monterrey* *Río Grande*

Tampa
Macdill
Flori

**Gulf of
Mexico**

Key W

San Luis Potosi
Aguascalientes Tampico
León
Querétaro
Tuxpan
Morelia
Toluca ■Mexico City *Veracruz*
Puebla
Bahia **MEXICO**
Acapulco
Coatzacoalcos

Mérida

Mariel
Havana

Ca
Isl
to

Salina Cruz

Chiapas

Usumacinta
Grijalva

border dispute to 1986

Belize City
■Belmopan
BELIZE
(British Honduras)
1981 independent
Puerto Cortes

to United States

**PACIFIC
OCEAN**

1954, ✳
1967–80 ✳ Puerto Barrios
Quetzaltenango
Puerto Madero Guatemala
Champerico City
to United States & Mexico
GUATEMALA
1954 US intervention
Acajutla
EL SALVADOR
1979–91 US & Israeli aid
to fight FMNLF guerrillas
to United States & Mexico

from 1981 insurgency
campaigns by US-
backed Contras

Tela La Ceiba
HONDURAS

Tegucigalpa

San Jose ✳1979
San
Salvador
La Unión **NICARAGUA**
Corinto ✳Esteli
León ■Managua
Lake
Nicaragua
Los Chiles

COSTA RICA
Caldera ✳San
José
1948, 1955
David
Puerto Armuelles

Cabo Grac
1957 border
Puerto Cab

San Juan de
Puerto Lim
Co
How
P/
198

Esmeral

Legend

- state borders
- disputed border
- ▢ British territory, 1941
- ▢ Dutch territory, 1941
- ▢ French territory, 1941
- ▢ United States territory, 1941
- ▢ country experiencing intervention
  by the United States
- ▢ Organization for Petroleum Exporting
  Countries (OPEC)
- ◯ United States blockade of Cuba from 1962
- ✳ civil war
- ● Contra base area
- ● Sandinista base
- ✈ United States air base
- ⊗ United States naval base
- ◉ Cuban missile site, 1962
- ↘ principal port
- ◯ coalfield
- ⛰ oilfield
- ── oil pipeline
- ➤ major migration since 1945

Nassau
BAHAMAS
1973 independent

rick

Miami
mestead

nfuegos
Bay of Pigs
961 US backed
bortive invasion
CUBA
Camagüey

Santiago
de Cuba
Guantánamo Bay
to United States

ited States
JAMAICA
1962 independent
Kingston
1972–80

to Canada

to Canada & Britain

to United States

Turks &
Caicos Islands
to Britain

*ATLANTIC
OCEAN*

Caribbean Sea

los

Puerto Plata
Santiago
HAITI
1994 US invasion
Port-au-Prince
DOMINICAN REPUBLIC
1965–66 US peacekeeping force
Santo
Domingo
La
Romana

Ramey
San
Juan
Roosevelt
Rhoads
Puerto Rico
to United States
Virgin Islands
to United States

Virgin
Islands
to Britain
Anguilla
to Britain

St Martin
to France & Netherlands
St Barthélemy
to France

Basseterre
ST KITTS
& NEVIS
1983 independent
St John's
ANTIGUA &
BARBUDA
1981 independent

Montserrat
to Britain

Basse-Terre
Guadeloupe
to France

Roseau
DOMINICA
1978 independent

Fort-de-France
Martinique
to France

to United States
Castries
ST LUCIA
1979 independent

to United States
ST VINCENT &
THE GRENADINES
1979 independent
Kingstown
1945, 1961–64

Bridgetown
BARBADOS
1966 independent
to Britain

GRENADA
1974 independent,
1983 US invasion
St George's

to Britain

Santa Marta
Barranquilla
Cartagena
Covenas

Albrook
Panama City
A
sion

Maracaibo
Puerto Cabello
Barquisimeto
Valencia
*Lake
Maracaibo*
Caracas
Petare
La Guaira
Maracay
Cumana
Guanta
Maturin

Port of
Spain
TRINIDAD
& TOBAGO
1962 independent

to United States

Cúcuta
San Christobal
Apure
VENEZUELA
1945, 1961–64
Ciudad Bolivar
Orinoco
Ciudad Guayana
Puerto Ordaz

Georgetown
New Amsterdam
Paramaribo
GUYANA
(British Guiana)
1966 independent
Nieuw
Nickerie
Nieuw
Amsterdam
Cayenne

to Netherlands

Bucaramanga
Medellin
COLOMBIA
1948–58
Manizales
Pereira
Ibagué
Bogota
Cali
Buenaventura
Cauca
Meta
1993 oil
reserves found
Guaviare

border disputed by Venezuela
1963–83
Cuyuni
Caroni
Essequibo

SURINAME
(Dutch Guiana)
1975 independent
French
Guiana
to France

border disputed
by Suriname

Orinoco

co
Pasto

Quito

ECUADOR
drew from OPEC

Aruba
to Netherlands
Netherlands
Antilles
to Netherlands

Central America and the Caribbean

All eight states of Central America, together with several islands of the Caribbean, have suffered from similar problems in the later 20th century. All had subsistence agriculture, unfair land distribution, and a deprived native peasant class. Tax evasion by the wealthy was endemic, and labor-intensive industries were lacking.

The states were too poor to fund welfare sufficiently to prevent political revolt, so political violence and state repression were commonplace. Aid (overwhelmingly from the United States) tended to prop up military leaders committed to anti-Communist policies, despite frequent corruption and human rights abuses.

Castro in Cuba

Before its revolution, Cuba was dominated by United States interests, with U.S. Marines stationed at their Guantánamo Bay base. Fidel Castro's successful revolution in 1959 led to hostility from the United States. The Soviet Union gave Castro support, especially after the American-supported but abortive counter-coup at the Bay of Pigs in 1961. The following year, Soviet ballistic missiles were stationed on the island, and eastern and southern United States lay within their range. U.S. president Kennedy imposed a naval blockade on the islands and even considered invasion, a step that seemed would inevitably lead to nuclear war. When Soviet leader Khrushchev removed the missiles, the threat of invasion was lifted, but the Soviet Union continued to support Cuba's economy and to fund its welfare state. However, Cuba went into decline after 1990 and faced U.S. sanctions.

Guerilla revolts

The United States feared that guerrilla revolts in Nicaragua, El Salvador, Guatemala, and Honduras would bring those countries under Soviet control. Cuban guerrillas were active in El Salvador, training rebels and fomenting strikes in 1976. In response, the army took over the government and killed thousands of civilian suspects. A similar cycle of events occurred in Guatemala. In Nicaragua, Sandinista guerrillas set up a Marxist–Leninist state in 1979. This was subverted by U.S.-trained rightwing Contra guerrillas; and in 1990 Sandinista leader Daniel Ortega was voted out of office. Mexico, the richest country in the region thanks to its reserves of oil, had few law and order problems, although the population quadrupled from 1940 and a recession hit in 1984. A Zapatista revolt in Chiapas province was crushed 10 years later.

Curriculum Context

Students should focus on the way political and economic conflict between the United States and the Soviet Union affected countries such as Guatemala.

U.S. intervention in the Caribbean

The United States intervened in the internal affairs of several Caribbean islands, again prompted by fear of Communism. The Dominican Republic was invaded by paratroopers in 1965, Grenada in 1983, and Haiti (the first Caribbean state to gain its independence) in 1994. Another United States intervention was to arrest on charges of drugs smuggling the president of Panama, Manuel Noriega, in 1989.

West Indies independence

In 1958–62 a federation of West Indian states was tried but failed, after which most became independent or chose to remain as British dependencies. In the 1950s, Britain actively sought immigrants from the West Indies, but curtailed this in 1962. Jamaica faced overpopulation, unemployment, and racial tension, but its educational programs and tourist attractions improved job opportunities. Trinidad and Tobago, richly endowed with oil and natural gas, suffered from a high birth rate, strikes, and sabotage due to Black Power groups and embittered Asians working on sugar plantations. Belize, a former British colony, was the last Central American country to gain independence.

Black Power

Political movement with its roots among blacks in the United States in the late 1960s, with a range of political goals including fighting racial oppression.

The Making of the Soviet Union

In the first quarter of the 20th century, revolution transformed Russia from a country under czarist rule to the Union of Soviet Socialist Republics, governed by the Communist Party.

SWEDEN

GERMANY

LITHUANIA
1940 to USSR

Danzig

Vienna

to Germany

Warsaw

POLAND

SLOVAKIA

HUNGARY

YUGOSLAVIA

Danube

ROMANIA

Romanians

BULGARIA

Istanbul

French Nikolayev

Odessa

Sevastopol

Simferopol

TURKEY

Black Sea

Euphrates

Tigris

Armenia
1918–21
independent

Batumi

Tbilisi

Georgia
1918–21
independent

Azerbaijan
1918–20 independent

Tabriz

Baku

British

British Caspian Sea

Tehran

IRAN

AFGHANISTAN

Kabul

Herat

Kushka

Mery

Samarkand

Ashkhabad

Bukhara

Tashkent

Frunze

Alma-Ata

T I E N

Krasnovodsk

Anu Dar'ya

Aral
Sea

Kazalinsk

Tallinn

LATVIA
1940 to USSR

ESTONIA
1940 to USSR

FINLAND
1917 independent

Murmansk

Riga

Lithuania

Latvia

Pskov

Leningrad
(Petrograd)

Archangel

Minsk

Belorussia
1919–21 independent

Shenkursk

Zhitomir

Smolensk

Kiev

Ukraine
1917–20 independent

Kaluga

Orel

Moscow

Kotlas

Poltava

Kharkov

Gorki

Yekaterinoslav

Voronezh

Tambov

Kazan

Gorki

Rostov

Mariupol

Novocherkassk

Saratov

Simbirsk

Kolchak
1918–19

Perm
(Molotov)

Novorossisk

Stalingrad

Samara
(Kuybyshev)

Ufa

Yekater
(Sverdlo

Cossacks,
Ukrainians,
White Russians

Cossacks

Orenburg

Chelyabinsk

URAL

Astrakhan

Magnitogorsk

Guryev

Legend

- ——— western frontier of Russian empire, 1914
- ⚑ principal town where Bolsheviks seized power, Nov–Dec 1917
- ▨ area controlled by Bolsheviks, Aug 1918
- ➤ advance of anti-Bolshevik armies, 1918–20
- ◯ area controlled by Bolsheviks, Oct 1919
- ——— border of temporarily independent area
- ➤ Japanese Siberian expedition, 1918–22
- ▦ Union of Soviet Socialist Republics, 1939
- ——— border, 1939
- ➤ Russian campaign, 1939
- ▨ main area of collectivization
- ◯ area under *gulag* administration
- ● new town founded 1925–38
- ⛏ oilfield
- ≈ hydroelectric power station
- ——— railroad

Novaya
Zemlya

New Siberian Islands

Wrangel Island

Vorkuta

Novyy Port

Nordvik

Ambarchik

Dubinka
Norilsk
Igarka

Tiksi

Kolymskaya

Anadyr

bolsk

UNION OF SOVIET
SOCIALIST REPUBLICS
from 1923

Magadan

Tomsk
Maklakovo

Novosibirsk

Krasnoyarsk

Lena

Yenisey

Ob

Stalinsk

*Sea of
Okhotsk*

Petropavlovsk

Cheremkhovo

Far Eastern
Republic
1920–22 independent

Magdagachi

Nikolaevsk

1925 to Russia

*Lake
Baykal*

Irkutsk
Ulan Ude
Chita

Komsomolsk

Aleksandrovsk

Sakhalin

Sovetskaya Gavan
Khabarovsk

Ulan Bator

MONGOLIA
1924 Communist state under
Russian influence

Manchuria
Harbin

Kuril Islands

Gobi Desert

Yellow

Mukden
(Shenyang)

Vladivostok

Sea of Japan

Beijing

Lushun
(Port Arthur)

Korea
Chosen from 1910
to Japan

Tokyo
JAPAN

*NORTH
PACIFIC
OCEAN*

Lanzhou

CHINA

*Yellow
Sea*

The Making of the Soviet Union

World War I imposed unbearable social and economic strain on Russia. The czar, who had assumed personal command of the armed forces in 1915, was held responsible for many of the failures of the war, and abdicated following a revolution in Petrograd in March (February in the Russian calendar) 1917.

Bolshevik

Member of majority Social Democratic Party (the "Reds") in Russia, comprising the proletariat (workers) who struggled against and overthrew the bourgeoisie (middle classes).

The provisional government's decision to continue the war, combined with fear of counterrevolution, led to increasing radicalization. Local soviets—committees of workers, soldiers, and sailors—sprang up in industrial areas. Many were dominated by radical socialist parties, among whom the Bolsheviks (led by Vladimir Ilych Lenin) won growing influence. In November (October) 1917, the Bolsheviks overthrew the government.

Creation of the USSR

The Bolsheviks were heavily outnumbered in the Constituent Assembly by the Socialist Revolutionaries representing the peasantry, so Lenin dissolved the Assembly and a bloody civil war began. Non-Bolshevik socialists, liberals, aristocrats, ethnic minorities, and the peasantry opposed the regime, and several foreign powers intervened, but anti-Bolshevik forces were too divided geographically and politically to succeed. Nineteen independent governments formed but the Bolsheviks (soon to be called Communists) recaptured the Ukraine, Caucasus, and Siberia. They ceded territory to Poland and recognized the independence of the Baltic states, but in 1923 created the Union of Soviet Socialist Republics (USSR), comprising the republics of Russia, Ukraine, Belorussia, and Transcaucasia.

The Five Year Plan

When Lenin died in 1924, Joseph Stalin secured control of the state. In 1928 Stalin announced the first Five Year

Plan to make the USSR a modern economic power. Production grew quickly, especially in the heavy and defense industries, as old industrial centers were expanded and new ones created in remote regions. Stalin ordered the collectivization of agriculture to provide sufficient grain to support a massive program of industrialization. Private trade was abolished and peasants forced to work on collective farms. Millions of peasants opposing collectivization were deported to the gulag. With insufficient food in the country, famine ensued, resulting in around 14.5 million deaths.

Purges

Industrial development was undermined by the purges that Stalin unleashed in 1934. "Subversives" (in the first instance, old Bolsheviks) appeared in show trials, were convicted of fantastic crimes and shot, while millions of others faced deportation to the gulag. Stalin's war with his own population extended across the Soviet Union as he sought scapegoats for the failures of collectivization and industrialization to achieve the targets set out in the Plan. Fear and suspicion led to mass denunciations and the decimation of the upper levels of bureaucracy and Party. By 1938 a purge of the army and navy began and the country lost most of its officer corps.

The USSR in World War II

In 1939 Stalin agreed the Nazi–Soviet pact with Hitler and occupied eastern Poland and the Baltic states. Stalin apparently believed that Hitler would not invade Russia until France and Britain were defeated; he also thought that fascism, which he saw as the highest form of capitalism, must presage the Communist revolution in Europe. In 1941, however, Hitler did invade. The Soviet Union was in a better position to resist than Russia had been in 1914, despite the purges. Stalin's policies were pursued at massive human cost and allowed the Communist Party to prevail.

Gulag

Network of forced labor camps or prisons in the Soviet Union, especially for political opponents to the Communist party.

Curriculum Context

The ways in which Stalin implemented decisions to collectivize and undergo the first Five Year Plan are important to understand the transformation in the 1920s and 1930s in the USSR.

The Decline of the Soviet Union

The Soviet Union emerged from
World War II a superpower, but
by the end of the 20th century the
former USSR had broken up into
independent states.

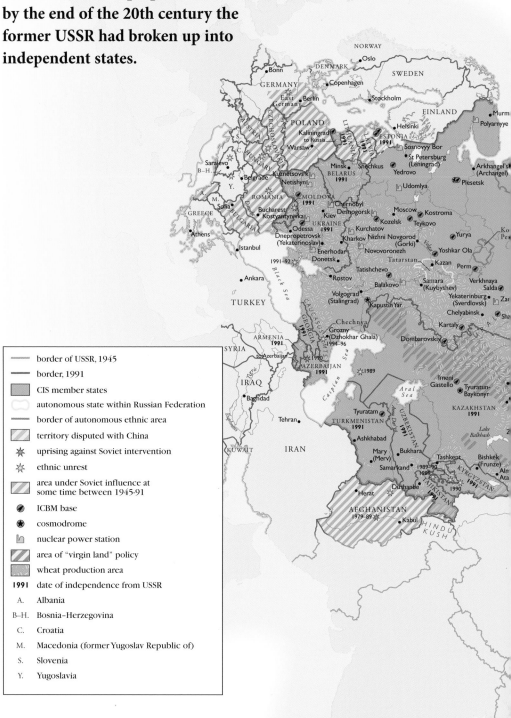

Legend:

- border of USSR, 1945
- border, 1991
- CIS member states
- autonomous state within Russian Federation
- border of autonomous ethnic area
- territory disputed with China
- ✳ uprising against Soviet intervention
- ✴ ethnic unrest
- area under Soviet influence at some time between 1945-91
- ⦸ ICBM base
- ✪ cosmodrome
- ⌂ nuclear power station
- area of "virgin land" policy
- wheat production area
- **1991** date of independence from USSR
- A. Albania
- B–H. Bosnia-Herzegovina
- C. Croatia
- M. Macedonia (former Yugoslav Republic of)
- S. Slovenia
- Y. Yugoslavia

Novaya
Zemlya

Drovyanaya

New Siberian Islands

Wrangel Island

ets

Taimyr
(Dolgan–Nenets)

Bilibino

Yamalo–
Nenets

Chukot

anty–
Mansi

RUSSIAN
FEDERATION
from 1991

Ob

Evenki

Koryak

Yenisey

Lena

Omsk

Yakutsk

Itatka

Magadan

Novosibirsk

Ob

Uzhur

Gladkaya
Krasnoyarsk

*Sea of
Okhotsk*

Kansk

Aleysk

Ust Ordyn
Buryat

*Lake
Baykal*

Sakhalin

Irkutsk

Chita

N SHAN

Agin
Buryat

Olovyannaya

Svobodnyy

Kuril Islands

Ulan
Bator

Birobijan
Jewish Autonomous
Region

Khabarovsk

Hami

MONGOLIA

Gobi Desert

CHINA

Harbin

Vladivostok

*Sea of
Japan*

Yellow

Mukden

Beijing

NORTH
KOREA

Pyongyang

JAPAN

*NORTH
PACIFIC
OCEAN*

Seoul

Tokyo

SOUTH
KOREA

The Decline of the Soviet Union

The German army advanced far into Russia, but the defiant Soviet forces fought back and advanced to Berlin by April 1945. World War II cost the USSR 20 million lives, but it took back the lands it had lost in 1918, liberated most of east Europe, then incorporated the region into what was effectively an empire. In 1949 it became a nuclear power.

Soviet agricultural production was costly and weak, bureaucracy was rampant in the state and industry, and order (especially over ethnic minorities) was enforced by terror. The Red Army took several years to put down partisan armies in Ukraine and Poland, while the annexed Baltic states were also hostile to Soviet rule. Stalin dealt with resurgent nationalism by deporting several subject nationalities for alleged collaboration. Many people, including members of the Politburo, greeted Stalin's death in 1953 with relief.

A new era

Many political prisoners were freed shortly after and, when Nikita Khrushchev emerged as the new Soviet head in 1955, he tried to rectify other problems of the Soviet Union. Khrushchev sought to improve the sluggish economy by producing consumer goods and the bureaucratic administration by decentralizing economic planning. In terms of foreign policy, two failures were the Cuban missile crisis and the Sino-Soviet split. Preparing for the possibility of war with both NATO and China, and financing heavy industry and the space program simultaneously was a huge drain on Soviet resources. Khrushchev could not remedy the problems of agriculture. Artificial fertilizers increased the yield of existing farms and helped cultivate untilled soil—the "virgin lands" campaign. Despite initial successes, the overfarming of land led to poor harvests and soil erosion; in 1963 the USSR was

Politburo

Short for "Political Bureau," the term Politburo describes the chief executive and political committee of the Communist Party.

Curriculum Context

An important aspect of interactions between the superpowers was their rivalry over the development of new military, nuclear, and space technology.

forced to import grain from the United States and Canada. Shortly thereafter, Khrushchev was deposed in a coup.

Going into reverse

His successor, Leonid Brezhnev, reversed Khrushchev's administrative policies. Corruption became endemic and growth rates slowed. The climate of international détente fostered in the 1970s evaporated with the Soviet invasion of Afghanistan and the election of the hawkish Ronald Reagan as president of the United States in 1980. Arms spending soared and the technological gap became ever more apparent. Grain subsidies, first paid to farmers by Khrushchev, were four times larger and exceeded the defense budget.

Curriculum Context

Students should analyze how such developments as the Soviet invasion of Afghanistan affected progress toward détente (easing tensions between East and West).

Opening up the Union

In 1985 Mikhail Gorbachev took over. His aims were to reduce spending on arms and introduce reform at home. *Glasnost* ("openness") and *perestroika* ("restructuring") became the key notes of his program but he underestimated the extent of internal tensions in the USSR. The relaxation of censorship allowed social, economic, and national grievances to surface. The crucial area of dispute proved to be the nationalities question. Liberals in the republics fixed on the idea of independence, the Baltic states and the Caucasus leading the way. At the same time the state was undermined by the opposition of Moscow-based reformist Boris Yeltsin.

Curriculum Context

Students should focus on why the Soviet and other Communist governments collapsed and the Soviet Union splintered into numerous states in the 1980s and early 1990s.

Elections did not provide a mandate for Gorbachev's reforms but rather took them further than he had envisaged and led to the dissolution of the Soviet Union. The Union was replaced by a loosely-based Commonwealth of Independent States (CIS). These faced drastic reorganization into market economies, and several—including the Russian Federation—faced civil war over nationality issues.

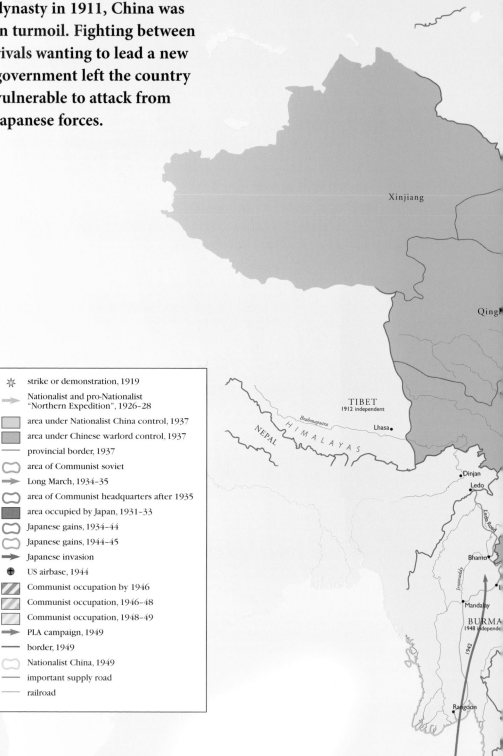

China 1911–1949

After the end of the Manchu dynasty in 1911, China was in turmoil. Fighting between rivals wanting to lead a new government left the country vulnerable to attack from Japanese forces.

Xinjiang

Qing

TIBET
1912 independent

Brahmaputra

NEPAL

H I M A L A Y A S

Lhasa

Dinjan
Ledo

Bhamo

Mandalay

BURMA
1948 independent

Rangoon

- ☼ strike or demonstration, 1919
- → Nationalist and pro-Nationalist "Northern Expedition", 1926–28
- ▢ area under Nationalist China control, 1937
- ▢ area under Chinese warlord control, 1937
- — provincial border, 1937
- ▢ area of Communist soviet
- → Long March, 1934–35
- ▢ area of Communist headquarters after 1935
- ▢ area occupied by Japan, 1931–33
- ▢ Japanese gains, 1934–44
- ▢ Japanese gains, 1944–45
- → Japanese invasion
- ⊕ US airbase, 1944
- ▨ Communist occupation by 1946
- ▨ Communist occupation, 1946–48
- ▨ Communist occupation, 1948–49
- → PLA campaign, 1949
- — border, 1949
- ▢ Nationalist China, 1949
- — important supply road
- — railroad

Lake Baykal

Chita

Nerchinsk

Blagoveshchensk

Khabarovsk

1931

Manchuria
(Manzhouguo)

Hailar

Xinqing

Nomonhan

Qiqihar

1939

1939

Inner Mongolian
Plateau

1931

Harbin

1931

Lake
Khanka

MONGOLIA
1911 independent,
1924 Communist state under
Russian influence

Changchun

Jilin

Gobi Desert

Chahar

1931

Vladivostok

Ordos
Desert

Zhangjiakou

Baotou

Suiyuan

Jehol
ceded to Japan 1933

Chengde

Shenyang
(Mukden)

Fushun

1948

Sea of
Japan

Datong 1949

Beijing

Tangshan

Anshan

Ningxia

Ghanzou

Yulin

Baoding

Tianjin

1937

Lushun
(Port Arthur)

Pyongyang

NORTH
KOREA
1948 independent

Yalu

Yan'an

Taiyuan

Shanxi

Zhili

Jinan

Dengzhou

Shandong Peninsula

1914

SOUTH
KOREA
1948 independent

Seoul

Lanzhou

Lake
Qinghai

Yellow

Handan

Anyang

Xinxiang

Shandong
Xuzhou
1948-49

Qingdao

Pusan

Yuncheng

Zhengzhou

Luoyang

1948

Kaifeng

Lianyungang

Yellow
Sea

Nagasaki

JAPAN

QIN
MTS

Gangu

Xi'an

Henan

Jiangsu

Taizhou

1932

Shaanxi

Nanyang

Huai

Anhui

Yangzhou

Zhenjiang

Shanghai

1937

Guanghua

Han

Nanjing

Wuxi

Suzhou

DABA MTS

Hubei

Wuhan

Hangzhou

Ningbo

East
China
Sea

Sichuan

Wanxian

Yichang

Yangzi

Zhejiang

Nanchong

Lichuan

Lake
Pengli

Chengdu

Hsikang

Chongqing

Nanchang

Ruijin
Islands
to Japan 1879

Luzhou

Lake
Dongting

Changsha

Jiangxi

Xichang

Zunyi

Hunan

Fuzhou

Matsu
1942

Jinsha

Yalong

Hengyang

Lingling

Suichuan

Juichin

Fujian

Taipei

Guizhou

Guilin

Xiamen
(Amoy)

Quemoy
1938

1942

Taiwan
to Japan until 1945

Burma Road

Kunming

Liuzhou

Guangdong

Shantou
(Swatow)

1939

Yunnan

Gejiu

Guangxi

Wuzhou

Guangzhou
(Canton)

Haifeng

South
China
Sea

Nanning

Macao
to Portugal

Hong Kong
to Britain

Vietnam

Lan Son

Xi

FRENCH
INDO-CHINA

Hanoi

Beihai

Zhanjiang

Laos

Haiphong

Haikou

AND
1939

1940

Mekong

1941

Hainan
1938-39 to Japan,
1945 to Nationalist China,
1950 to Communist China

1941

China 1911–1949

The sudden but relatively bloodless revolution of 1911 led to the abdication of the Manchu emperor; the new republic was headed first by Sun Yixian (Sun Yat-sen) and then by Yuan Shikai (from 1912). Yuan used terror to consolidate his power and banned the Guomindang (KMT—Nationalist Party).

The disillusioned Sun Yixian sought refuge in Japan, which was allied with Britain and France against Germany. Japanese troops landed on the Shandong peninsula and demanded concessions from Yuan. Yuan, seeing China threatened by Japan, planned a new dynasty with himself as emperor. After another rebellion, Yuan retreated to Beijing and died in 1916.

Curriculum Context

Students studying China should focus on the promise and failure of China's 1911 republican revolution to address the country's political, economic, and social problems.

China in chaos

China drifted into chaos. Warlords pillaged the countryside. When floods or famine struck, there was no administration to alleviate the effects. Japan kept its foothold in Shandong, while foreign governments held concessions along the coast and the Yangtze river. Chinese sovereignty and territorial rights were ignored. Students receptive to the teachings of Marx led nationalist demonstrations and helped form the Chinese Communist Party (CCP) in Shanghai.

New leaders

The Soviet Union supported both the CCP and Sun Yixian's Guomindang and, after Sun's death, Soviet and Communist influence on the Guomindang increased. Jiang Jieshi (Chiang Kai-shek), Sun's successor, built up a powerful base in Guangdong and moved against the warlords in the north and the Communists. The survivors fled into Jiangxi province. In 1934 Jiang forced them to leave Jiangxi. They began their Long March to Yan'an in Shaanxi province, during which Mao Zedong emerged as the CCP leader.

Long March

Historic 6,000-mile (9,600-km) journey from Jiangxi to the northern Shaanxi Province, undertaken by Chinese Communist forces to escape the Guomindang.

The Japanese in China

Japan had invaded Manchuria in 1931 and launched a fullscale invasion of China in 1937. Jiang shifted his capital from Nanjing to Chongqing. Since he could hold out as long as he received supplies from western Allies, Japan moved into French Indo-China to cut the rail link with Chongqing. In the north Mao Zedong organized a guerrilla war against the Japanese but the fighting remained local. When the Americans built up a bomber force in west China, the Japanese overran a great deal of China in an attempt to destroy U.S. bases.

The People's Republic of China

At the end of World War II the Japanese surrendered and the Communists and the Nationalists began to compete for Manchuria. At this point, however, United States sanctions terminated all aid to both sides. Inflation, corruption, and food shortages soon wrecked civilian morale and despair transferred to the Nationalist soldiers. In 1948, the Communist People's Liberation Army (PLA) moved south. The PLA crossed the Yangtze in 1949 and, as Nationalist armies crumbled, began a triumphal march through the cities of southern China. By September the civil war was virtually over. Mao Zedong declared victory over foreign and domestic enemies, and the establishment of the People's Republic of China with himself as chairman of the central government.

Curriculum Context

Students should focus on the struggle between the Guomindang and the Communists in the context of political fragmentation, economic transformation, and Japanese imperialism.

The Guomindang in Taiwan

Jiang Jieshi shifted his power base to Chengdu in 1949 and abandoned the mainland, transferring "Nationalist China" to the island of Taiwan, where he remained as president until his death in 1975. Apart from Taiwan and some offshore islands, China was now under the control of the CCP.

The Soviet Union and the Communist bloc recognized the People's Republic, as did Britain in 1950. The United States, though, remained hostile and refused to allow China's admission to the United Nations, insisting until 1971 that Taiwan retain China's seat on the Security Council.

Japan and Asia

In Asia the first half of the 20th century was characterized by the diminishing power of the colonial countries and an expansion of Japanese interests.

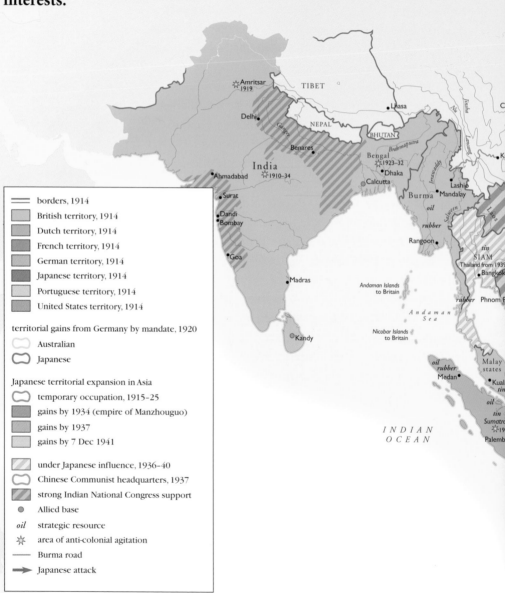

borders, 1914

British territory, 1914

Dutch territory, 1914

French territory, 1914

German territory, 1914

Japanese territory, 1914

Portuguese territory, 1914

United States territory, 1914

territorial gains from Germany by mandate, 1920

Australian

Japanese

Japanese territorial expansion in Asia

temporary occupation, 1915–25

gains by 1934 (empire of Manzhouguo)

gains by 1937

gains by 7 Dec 1941

under Japanese influence, 1936–40

Chinese Communist headquarters, 1937

strong Indian National Congress support

Allied base

oil strategic resource

area of anti-colonial agitation

Burma road

Japanese attack

TIBET

Lhasa

Delhi

NEPAL

Amritsar 1919

BHUTAN

Benares

Brahmaputra

Bengal 1923–32

Dhaka

India 1910–34

Ahmadabad

Calcutta

Lashio

Surat

Burma

Mandalay

Dandi

Bombay

oil

rubber

Goa

Rangoon

tin

SIAM

Thailand from 1939

Madras

Bangkok

Andaman Islands to Britain

rubber Phnom P

Andaman Sea

Nicobar Islands to Britain

Kandy

oil
rubber

Malay states

Medan

Kuala
tin

oil

tin

Sumatra

INDIAN OCEAN

Palemba

- Chita
- Manzhouli
- Khalkin-Gol ☆ 1939

UNION OF SOVIET SOCIALIST REPUBLICS

Amur

Manchuria 1931 Japanese occupation, 1932 republic of Manzhouguo, 1934 empire of Manzhouguo

- Khabarovsk
- Harbin

Sakhalin
Karafuto

coal

Kuril Islands

- Vladivostok

Chahar

Jehol 1933 to Manzhouguo

- Mukden (Shenyang)
- Chang-ku Feng 1938

oil

Hokkaido

coal

to Pearl Harbor (Hawaii), Dec 1941

Suiyuan 1938

Marco Polo Bridge 1937

1938

- Beijing
- Tianjin

coal

- Pyongyang

Sea of Japan

Shanxi *Zhili* 1938

- Yulin
- Yan'an

Korea
Chosen, 1910-45

Lushun (Port Arthur)
- Dalian (Dairen)
- Weihaiwei 1930 to China 1938 to Japan
- Seoul
- Pyongyang

oil

JAPAN

- Nagoya
- Tokyo

Honshu

coal

- Kyoto
- Pusan
- Shimonoseki

Shandong

coal

- Qingdao 1914 to Japan
- Kaifeng 1938
☆ Tai'erzhuang 1938

Yellow Sea

iron

- Nagasaki

coal

Shikoku

- Xi'an

Kyushu

- Nanjing 1937
☆ 1925
- Wuhan 1938

☆ Shanghai 1937

East China Sea

CHINA
☆ 1919-45

- Changsa
- Wenzhou

NORTH PACIFIC OCEAN

Bonin Islands to Japan

Tongking 1940 under Japanese occupation

- Xiamen (Amoy)
- Fuzhou
- Taipei

Ryukyu Islands

- Okinawa

Daito Islands to Japan

Volcano Islands to Japan

Marcus Island to Japan

- Guangzhou (Canton)
- Shantou (Swatow)
- Tainan

Taiwan

- Hong Kong to Britain
- Macao to Portugal

1939

Haiphong

Hainan

Annam 1941 under Japanese occupation

- Luzon
- Manila

Philippine Sea

Mariana Islands

South China Sea

Philippines

China 1930

Saigon

- Iloilo
- Cebu

Guam to United States

Yap Islands

Caroline Islands

COCHIN CHINA 1941 under Japanese occupation

- Palawan
- Mindanao
- Zamboanga
- Davao

rubber

Palau Islands

British North Borneo

- Bandar Seri Begawan (Brunei)
- Sandakan

rubber

- Brunei
- oil oil

Celebes Sea

Halmahera

- Kuching

Sarawak

rubber

- Jayapura (Hollandia)
- Wewak

New Ireland

- Banjarmasin

Borneo

oil

German New Guinea

Bougainville

rubber

- Celebes

oil

Dutch New Guinea

New Britain

Batavia

Java Sea

Banda Sea

- Ceram

bauxite ☆1926 oil Surabaya

Java

rubber

Dutch East Indies (Netherlands India)

rubber

- Dili Portuguese Timor

Timor

New Guinea

Arafura Sea

Territory of Papua to Australia

- Port Moresby

Coral Sea

AUSTRALIA

New

Japan and Asia

The Russo–Japanese War of 1904–05 gave Japan protectorate authority over Korea and the lease of Chinese territory in south Manchuria. From these bases the army looked to consolidate its influence in Manchuria and north China. By this time, a new and increasingly militant anti-imperialist nationalism was developing among young Chinese people.

Nationalist movements grew elsewhere in Asia too, for example in India and Vietnam. In China, resentment after 1905 was focused on Japan as the other western powers were preoccupied with European politics and hoped merely to hold onto their Asian interests. Tokyo's decision to enter World War I was driven as much by interests in China—where the Manchu dynasty had fallen in 1911—as by the desire to help its ally, Britain. In August 1914 Japan took over territories in Shandong and eventually occupied the whole province.

Colonial decline

The end of the war marked a turning point for the European powers in east Asia: Britain, France, the Netherlands, and, to a lesser extent, Portugal. All had been weakened by the war and the League of Nations (1919) adopted a policy generally critical of colonialism. Britain began to explore ways to enable Asian colonies to achieve commonwealth status (like Australia) or self-governing dominion status (like New Zealand, since 1907). The Dutch began to consider passing power to native populations, too.

Nationalist movements

Nationalist movements in the colonies gained impetus during the worldwide depression of the 1930s. In India, the Indian National Congress, led by Jawaharlal Nehru and Mohandas "Mahatma" Gandhi, organized a mass self-rule movement in the 1920s and 1930s. Burma

Curriculum Context

An important aspect of nationalist movements in Asia is the way in which the Depression affected colonial peoples and contributed to the growth of nationalist sentiments.

separated from India and was given a form of responsible government in 1937. The Dutch East Indies experienced a Communist uprising in 1926–27, and French Indo-China also saw Communist-inspired strikes and rural unrest. Neither the French nor the Dutch made significant concessions, and—except in India—the nationalist movements appeared divided and unable to make a lasting impression. In 1935 the United States, however, promised independence for its own colony in the Philippines within 10 years.

Japanese interests in east Asia

From 1931 Japan pursued an aggressive policy toward the Nationalist government in China, which was already engaged in civil war with Chinese Communists. Japan's massacre of civilians in the Nationalist cities of Shanghai and Nanjing drew criticism from the west. In 1939 Japanese forces landed in French Indo-China to cut off supply routes to the Nationalists and, after France fell to Hitler in 1940, the Japanese occupied most of the colony. Politically, the Japanese exploited anti-European feeling among the nationalist groups, promising economic prosperity under the Greater East Asian Co-Prosperity Sphere. Some were persuaded by this message; others saw it as Japanese imperialism.

Steps toward war

The United States proposed an embargo on imports from Japan in 1937 and banned exports to Japan of scrap iron (1940) and oil (1941). The British and Dutch supported the oil embargo, whereupon Japan looked to the oil-rich Dutch East Indies, and the tin- and rubber-rich British colonies of Burma and Malaya as sources of raw materials. Japan realized that aggression against these would lead to war with the United States, but when diplomacy failed it attacked the U.S. naval base at Pearl Harbor and the Philippines in December 1941, and swept down into Dutch and British southeast Asia.

World War II in Asia

During World War II, Japan extended its political and economic interest and influence in southeast Asia, before being forced to surrender by America's atomic bombs.

N

Chita

Hailar

Chang
co

Ansh

Beijing

Tianjin

Jinan

coal

coal

Qir

Kaifeng

Y

Lanzhou

Yan'an
1937–45

Yellow

Xi'an
1937–45

CHINA

Chengdu
Sept 1944

Nanjing

Wuhan

Yangzi

TIBET

Lhasa

BHUTAN

Chongqing
1937–45

Changsa
Sept–Oct 1941,
Dec 1941–Jan 1942

W.

NEPAL

Thimphu

June 1944

Fuzh

Kathmandu

Kohima
Apr–June 1944

Yunnan

Kunming
1937–45

Guilin
Sept 1944

Xiamen

Fuzhc

Southeast
Asian Forces

Imphal
Mar–June 1944

1944–45

Shantou

Taiv

Guangzhou

Tain

India
to Britain

Calcutta

Burma

Mandalay

oil

Hanoi
Haiphong
coal

Hong Kong
Dec 1941

194

1942

Vishakhapatnam
Apr 1942

Arakan

rubber

Hainan

Luzon
Jan–Jun 1945

194

Kakinada
Apr 1942

Bay of
Bengal

Rangoon

tin

THAILAND

BATAAN

M

Bangkok

1941

French
Indo-China

Corregidor
Jan–May 1942

Andaman
Islands

Oct 194

Trincomalee
Apr 1942

rubber

Phnom Penh

rubber

Saigon

Palawan

1945

Colombo
Apr 1942

Bay of Bengal
Apr 1942

Nicobar
Islands

1941

British
North
Borneo

Sandakar

oil
rubber

Malaya

1942

Brunei

rubber
oil

Tarakan

Medan

Kuala Lumpur
Feb 1942

tin

Kuching

Sarawak

Brunei

Sumatra

oil

Singapore

tin

Borneo

oil

1945

Palembang

Balikpapan
rubber

Celebes

Batavia

Java
Sea

Banjarmasin

Java Sea
Feb 1942

Macassar

bauxite

Surabaya

Dutch Ea

Java

oil rubber

Broome,
Mar 1942

═══	borders, 7 Dec 1941
⬭	Japanese occupied territory, 7 Dec 1941
⬭	maximum extent of Japanese occupied territory, June 1942
----	intended eastern perimeter of Japanese territory
▦	Japanese occupied territory, 6 Aug 1945
▦	Japanese occupied territory, Sep 1945
▦	Allied territory, June 1942
▦	Nationalist Chinese or warlord territory
▨	Communist Chinese territory, 1937
→	Japanese advance, with date
→	Allied advance, with date
→	Russian advance, 9 Aug 1945
⚑	Japanese base, June 1942
♨	Japanese air strike outside occupied territory
♨	US bombing raids on Japan, 1942–45
☈	nuclear air strike, Aug 1945
⊗	Japanese victory
⊗	Allied victory
oil	strategic resource vital to Japan

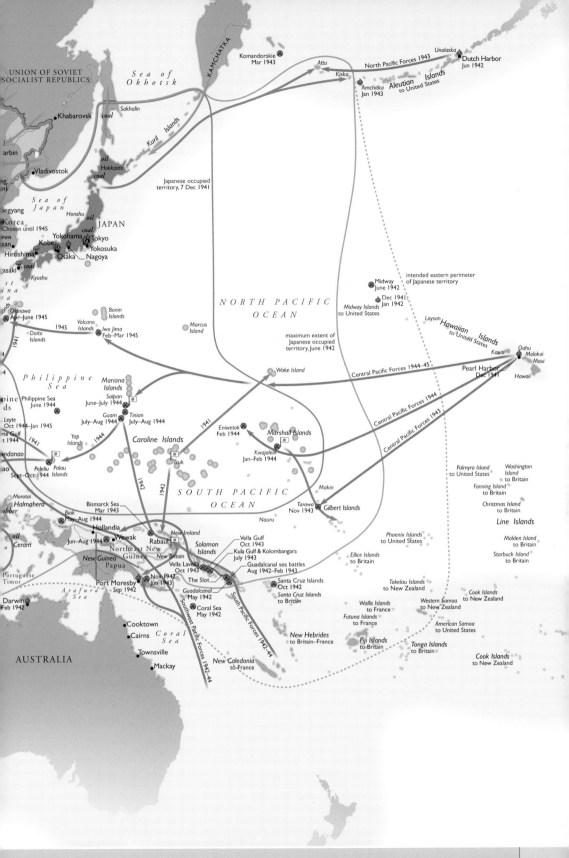

UNION OF SOVIET
SOCIALIST REPUBLICS

Sea of Okhotsk

KAMCHATKA

Komandorskie
Mar 1943

Unalaska

Dutch Harbor
Jun 1942

North Pacific Forces 1943

Attu

Kiska

Amchitka
Jan 1943

Aleutian   Islands
to United States

•Khabarovsk

Sakhalin

coal

Kuril   Islands

oil

•Vladivostok

Hokkaido

coal

Japanese occupied
territory, 7 Dec 1941

*Sea of
Japan*

Honshu

oil

arbin

Korea
Chosen until 1945

JAPAN

coal

ongyang

ron

•Yokohama •Tokyo

an

•Kobe• Yokosuka

•Hiroshima   Osaka•   Nagoya

*NORTH PACIFIC
OCEAN*

Midway
June 1942

intended eastern perimeter
of Japanese territory

asaki

Kyushu

Dec 1941
Jan 1942

Midway Islands
to United States

Laysan

Hawaiian   Islands
to United States

t
na

Okinawa
Apr–June 1945

*Bonin
Islands*

1945

*Marcus
Island*

maximum extent of
Japanese territory, June 1942

Oahu

Kauai

Molokai
Maui

1941

*Volcano
Islands*

Iwo Jima
Feb–Mar 1945

*Daito
Islands*

Wake Island

Central Pacific Forces 1944–45

Pearl Harbor
Dec 1941

Hawaii

*Philippine
Sea*

Mariana
Islands

Saipan
June–July 1944

4

Philippine Sea
June 1944

1941

Guam
July–Aug 1944

Tinian
July–Aug 1944

Eniwetok
Feb 1944

Marshall Islands

Central Pacific Forces 1944

ne
ds

Leyte
Oct 1944–Jan 1945

te Gulf
1944

1941

*Yap
Islands*

Caroline Islands

Kwajalein
Jan–Feb 1944

Central Pacific Forces 1943

ndanao

ao

Peleliu
Sept–Oct 1944

Palau
Islands

1942

Truk

*SOUTH PACIFIC
OCEAN*

Makin

Palmyra Island
to United States

*Washington
Island*
to Britain

Morotai

Halmahera

1942

Tarawa
Nov 1943

Gilbert Islands

Fanning Island
to Britain

ubber

Biak
May–Aug 1944

Bismarck Sea
Mar 1943

Nauru

Christmas Island
to Britain

oil

Hollandia

New Ireland

Line Islands

a

Ceram

Jun–Aug 1944

•Wewak

Rabaul

Vella Gulf
Oct 1943

Phoenix Islands
to United States

Malden Island
to Britain

Portuguese
Timor

New Guinea

Northeast New
Guinea

New Britain

*Solomon
Islands*

Kula Gulf & Kolombangara
July 1943

Ellice Islands
to Britain

Starbuck Island
to Britain

Papua

Nov 1942
Jun 1943

New Guinea

The Slot

Vella Lavella
Oct 1943

Guadalcanal sea battles
Aug 1942–Feb 1943

•Port Moresby
Sep 1942

*Arafura
Sea*

Coral Sea
May 1942

Guadalcanal
May 1942

Santa Cruz Islands
Oct 1942

Santa Cruz Islands
to Britain

Wallis Islands
to France

Tokelau Islands
to New Zealand

Western Samoa
to New Zealand

Cook Islands
to New Zealand

Darwin
Feb 1942

South Pacific Forces 1942–44

Southwest Pacific Forces 1942–44

Futuna Islands
to France

American Samoa
to United States

•Cooktown

*Coral
Sea*

Fiji Islands
to Britain

Tonga Islands
to Britain

•Cairns

New Hebrides
to Britain–France

•Townsville

Cook Islands
to New Zealand

•Mackay

New Caledonia
to France

AUSTRALIA

World War II in Asia

In late 1941 the Japanese planned a series of synchronized attacks to secure control in the Pacific and Asia. Japanese leaders sought to create a defensive perimeter from the Kuril islands to the Dutch East Indies to contain all the oil, rubber, and rice Japan would need for survival, and promised a string of victories in the first six months.

Curriculum Context

It is important to understand the precipitating causes of the war and the reasons for early Japanese (and German) victories.

Battle of Midway

Sea battle fought June 4–6, 1942, near the Midway Islands in the Pacific Ocean; it was a major U.S. victory and gave Americans sea power over the Japanese.

Japan's prime minister Hideki Tojo and Isoroko Yamamoto, head of the navy, planned the surprise attack on the United States naval base of Pearl Harbor in Hawaii on December 7, 1941. The attack destroyed the U.S. Pacific battlefleet, but all the large aircraft carriers were at sea. The survival of these warships was to be of crucial significance. By the spring of 1942 Japan had taken the Philippines (attacked the same day as Pearl Harbor), ejected the Dutch from the East Indies, driven the British from Hong Kong, Malaya (including the great naval base of Singapore), and most of Burma, and forced the Americans to surrender Guam, Wake Island, Attu, and Kiska. At this point, Japan suffered a setback at the Battle of the Coral Sea, when they attempted to take the Allied base at Port Moresby on New Guinea (thus isolating Australia). Further advances across the Pacific were decisively halted when the imperial fleet was defeated by the U.S. Navy at the Battle of Midway.

Allied strategies in Asia

Allied strategy for the destruction of Japan's new empire depended upon the immense resources and manpower that the United States could bring to bear. The plan required the British, who had suffered during their long retreat in Burma, to block a Japanese invasion of India, undertake offensives in the Arakan, and recapture Rangoon, capital of Burma. They would have limited U.S. assistance and cooperation from

Chinese Nationalist armies from Yunnan. These forces came under a new southeast Asia command headed by Lord Louis Mountbatten. U.S. forces in the south and southwest Pacific under General Douglas MacArthur and Admiral William Halsey planned to retake New Guinea and the Solomons. Admiral Chester Nimitz would assemble fresh task forces at Pearl Harbor and attack Japanese-held islands in the central and north Pacific. Key bases would be established on the islands and in China for an air assault upon Japan.

Establishing U.S. bases

In the north Pacific, U.S. and Canadian troops attacked in the Aleutians and forced the Japanese back. In the central Pacific, U.S. Marines assaulted the tiny coral atoll of Tarawa, 5,000 kilometers (3,000 miles) from Japan. They wiped out its Japanese and Korean defenders, but only after three days of bitter fighting. After this experience, the Americans decided to ignore unimportant islands and bypass many Japanese bases. They fought and won the Battle of the Philippine Sea and then targeted Kwajalein and Eniwetok in the Marshalls. They went on to occupy Saipan, Guam, and Tinian, the bases from which in 1944–45 U.S. B-29 bombers undertook their raids on Japanese cities.

U.S. forces returned to the Philippines and fought the Battle of Leyte Gulf, during which the Japanese navy was effectively destroyed. The Battle of Iwo Jima, the fiercest of the war, provided the Americans with a base for their fighter aircraft capable of escorting bombers to Japan and back. About 500,000 troops were then committed to attack Okinawa; the Japanese defenders employed kamikaze aircraft and piloted bombs against American and British ships.

Allied advances

Before and during the Iwo Jima and Okinawa campaigns the Americans subjected Japan to constant

This photograph captures the moment when victorious Marines raised the American flag at the summit of Mt. Suribachi, the highest point of the island of Iwo Jima, on February 23, 1945, after a month of severe fighting.

and debilitating bombing. Tokyo, Nagoya, and Osaka were devastated and the Tokyo firestorm of May 1945 is considered to be the most destructive air raid in history. In the Philippines, the Battle of Luzon was still in progress and in Burma the British, Indian, African, Chinese, and U.S. troops, after great battles at Kohima and Imphal, were slowly pushing down the Irrawaddy toward Mandalay and Rangoon.

Japan surrenders

Despite near universal defeat, the Japanese had no desire to surrender and all sides anticipated a fight to the finish. Allied planning for an amphibious attack on Japan went ahead. Stalin promised that the Soviet Union would enter the war against Japan three months after the total surrender of Nazi Germany. President Harry S. Truman assessed the likely scale of casualties involved in an invasion (approximately one million fighting men), and compared this with the enemy civilian deaths that would result from the use of the new atomic bomb being tested in New Mexico. He chose the atomic weapon: the bombs fell on Hiroshima and Nagasaki in August 1945. After the first strike Stalin declared war and Soviet troops invaded Manchuria and Korea. As Japan reeled, carrier aircraft harried Honshu and Kyushu and a giant bombing raid savaged the remains of Tokyo.

On August 15, 1945, Emperor Hirohito asked the Japanese people to "endure the unendurable and suffer the insufferable." Japan formally signed the surrender document on the battleship USS *Missouri* on September 2, 1945.

Curriculum Context

Students should be able to explain how 20th-century technologies and scientific breakthroughs both benefited and imperiled humankind. The atomic bomb is a good example.

East Asia Since 1945

After World War II, countries in East Asia faced new conflicts, some against foreign powers for independence; others among rival factions within their own borders.

N

MONGOLIA

Ulan Bator
•Tsetserleg
Hai

PEOPLE'S
REPUBLIC
OF CHINA

Hohhot
Fangshan • Beijing
Tianjin
Dali
Taiyuan Shijiazhuang
Xining Ningxia Yan'an Linyi
Lanzhou Jinan
Xi'an Louyang Zhengzhou

Nanjing
Yangtze
Hanyang Wuhan
Chongqing Nanchang Wenzhou
Yibin
Weining Changsha
Guiyang Fuzhou
Kunming Guilin
Nanning Liuzhou Wuzhou Quemoy
Macao Guangzhou Tainan
to Portugal Hong Kong
to Britain

Islamabad

Xizang
(Tiber)
1950–59 Tibetan revolt
against Chinese,
1965 nominally autonomous
region of China

Tang Pass

PAKISTAN
West Pakistan
until 1971,
1947

1950

1962

Qamdo Chengdu
Chongqing

New
Delhi Thimphu
Kathmandu Lhasa•
Brahmaputra

NEPAL BHUTAN

INDIA
1947

Dhaka

BANGLADESH
(East Pakistan)
1947 to Pakistan,
1971

Calcutta•

Monywa Mandalay Dien Bien
Phu Hanoi Haiphong
North Vietnam
LAOS 1954, 1976 united
1954 as Vietnam
1953–73
Chiang
Mai
VIETNAM
Vientiane **1976** (united)
THAILAND Communist Da Nang
insurgency
from 1960s
Nakhon
Ratchasima South Vietnam
Bangkok 1954, 1975 to North Vietnam,
CAMBODIA 1976 united as Vietnam
1954 until 1975

Hainan

Paracel Islands
to China,
claimed by Vietnam

Manila

Sittwe•
Communist insurgency
from 1948

Rangoon•
Karen separatist
insurgency from 1948

BURMA
1948

*Bay of
Bengal*

Andaman Islands
to Britain,
1947 to India

SRI LANKA
Ceylon until 1972
1947

*INDIAN
OCEAN*

Phnom Penh
Ho Chi Minh City
(Saigon)

muslim insurgency
from 1960s

Nicobar Islands
to Britain,
1947 to India

*Andaman
Sea*

Hat Yai

1953–59 Islamic
rebellion
1958–59 anti-
Communist rebellion

George Town

Medan

MALAYSIA
1963

Sabah
1963 to Malaysia
Brunei
to Britain
Sarawak
1963 to Malaysia

Malaya
1957, 1963 to Malaysia
1948–60 Malayan
Emergency

Kuala
Lumpur

Kuching

Borneo

1946–49
Pekanbaru

Singapore
SINGAPORE
1963 to Malaysia,
1965
Pontianak Samarinda

Padang

Sumatra
Palembang

Balikpapan

Banjarmasin

Jakarta
(Batavia)
Bandung

Java

1946–49,
1951–58

1948 Communist
rebellion,
1965–66 Massacre of
the Communists

Java Sea Ujungpandang
(Makassar)

Surabaya
Bali

1946–49

1946–49

Cele

0 _____ 400 km
0 _____ 600 mi

Tonghua•
•Chongjin

PEOPLE'S
REPUBLIC
OF
CHINA

Chosan•
Dandong•
•Unsan
NORTH
KOREA
Pyongyang■

Hungnam
•Wonsan

*Sea of
Japan*

Timen
Yalu

armistice line 27 July
1953 (effective front
line from July 1951)
38th Parallel

Panmunjom•
Inchon• •Seoul

United States
X Corps,
Sep 1950

SOUTH
KOREA

Taejon•
•Taegu •Pohang

Mokpo• •Pusan

United States
Eighth Army

JAPAN

➤ North Korean advance, June–Sept 1950

➤ United Nations liberation force advance, July–Sept 1950

➤ Chinese and North Korean advance, Nov 1950–Jan 1951

— limit of North Korean advance, Aug–Sept 1950

— limit of United Nations advance, Nov 1950

— limit of Chinese and North Korean advance, Jan 1951

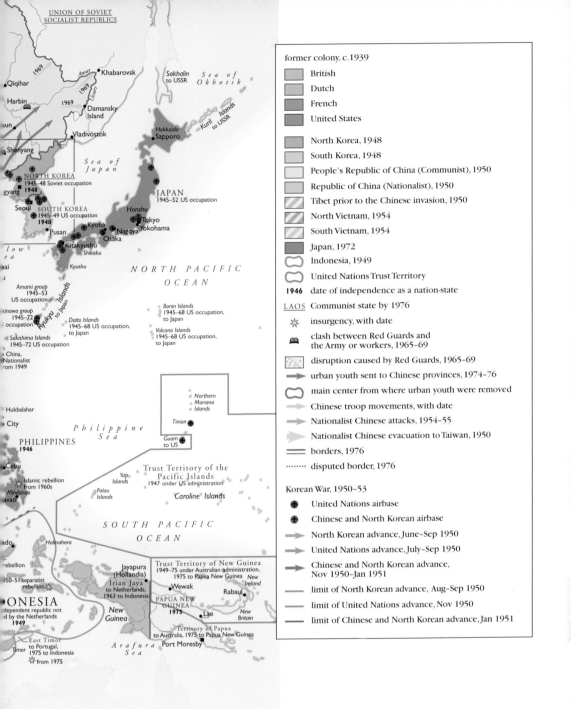

former colony, c.1939

British
Dutch
French
United States

North Korea, 1948
South Korea, 1948
People's Republic of China (Communist), 1950
Republic of China (Nationalist), 1950
Tibet prior to the Chinese invasion, 1950
North Vietnam, 1954
South Vietnam, 1954
Japan, 1972
Indonesia, 1949
United Nations Trust Territory
1946 date of independence as a nation-state
L̲A̲O̲S̲ Communist state by 1976
insurgency, with date
clash between Red Guards and the Army or workers, 1965-69
disruption caused by Red Guards, 1965-69
urban youth sent to Chinese provinces, 1974-76
main center from where urban youth were removed
Chinese troop movements, with date
Nationalist Chinese attacks, 1954-55
Nationalist Chinese evacuation to Taiwan, 1950
borders, 1976
disputed border, 1976

Korean War, 1950-53

United Nations airbase
Chinese and North Korean airbase
North Korean advance, June-Sep 1950
United Nations advance, July-Sep 1950
Chinese and North Korean advance, Nov 1950-Jan 1951
limit of North Korean advance, Aug-Sep 1950
limit of United Nations advance, Nov 1950
limit of Chinese and North Korean advance, Jan 1951

Map labels:

UNION OF SOVIET SOCIALIST REPUBLICS

Qiqihar
Harbin
Khabarovsk
1969
Amur
Ussuri
1969
Damansky Island
Vladivostok
Shenyang
Sakhalin to USSR
Sea of Okhotsk
Kuril Islands to USSR
Hokkaido
Sapporo
Sea of Japan
NORTH KOREA
1945-48 Soviet occupation
gyang
1948
Seoul
SOUTH KOREA
1945-49 US occupation
1948
Pusan
Kyoto
Nagoya
Osaka
Kitakyushu
Shikoku
Kyushu
JAPAN
1945-52 US occupation
Honshu
Tokyo
Yokohama

Amami group 1945-53 US occupation
kinawa group 1945-72 occupation
Sakishima Islands 1945-72 US occupation
China, Nationalist rom 1949

Ryukyu Islands to Japan

NORTH PACIFIC OCEAN

Bonin Islands 1945-68 US occupation, to Japan
Daito Islands 1945-68 US occupation, to Japan
Volcano Islands 1945-68 US occupation, to Japan

Hukbalahar
City
PHILIPPINES
1946
Cebu
Islamic rebellion from 1960s
Mindanao
avao

Philippine Sea

Northern Mariana Islands
Tinian
Guam to US

Trust Territory of the Pacific Islands 1947 under US administration

Yap Islands
Palau Islands
'Caroline' Islands

SOUTH PACIFIC OCEAN

ido
Halmahera
rebellion
950-51 separatist rebellion
ONESIA
dependent republic not d by the Netherlands 1949
East Timor to Portugal, 1975 to Indonesia
Timor from 1975

Jayapura (Hollandia)
Irian Jaya to Netherlands, 1963 to Indonesia
New Guinea

Trust Territory of New Guinea 1949-75 under Australian administration, 1975 to Papua New Guinea
Wewak
PAPUA NEW GUINEA
1975
Lae
New Ireland
Rabaul
New Britain

Territory of Papua to Australia, 1975 to Papua New Guinea
Port Moresby
Arafura Sea

East Asia Since 1945

The end of World War II left the United States dominant in east Asia but the Soviet Union was also moving strongly into the region. The Chinese civil wars were soon to be resolved, while the European colonies had been decisively altered by the experience of Japanese occupation and U.S. liberation.

In September 1945 U.S. forces, committed to preventing the spread of Communism, landed at Inchon in the former Japanese colony of Korea in response to the presence of Soviet troops in north Korea. No formula could be found for unifying the country and the United Nations approved an American plan to hold elections in the south. Syngman Rhee's Republic of Korea (South Korea) emerged in 1948, followed shortly by Kim Il Sung's Communist Democratic Republic of Korea (North Korea). The Soviet Union and United States withdrew in 1948 and 1949, respectively, leaving Korea deeply divided.

American influence in Japan

Many U.S. troops withdrew to Japan, where America was responsible for its military occupation and the repatriation of three million Japanese servicemen. The United States and its Commonwealth Allies met with unexpected cooperation from Japanese police and local officials. Emperor Hirohito remained, though only as titular ruler, and real power was in the hands of General MacArthur, Supreme Commander of Allied Powers. MacArthur introduced a democratic constitution, ensured that the United States shipped in adequate food supplies, and generally charmed the Japanese with his dignity and benevolence. The Japanese came to admire Americans and their way of life. By 1949 Japan was willingly drawn inside America's defensive perimeter.

Curriculum Context

Students may be asked to compare the impact of Soviet domination on Eastern Europe with changes that occurred in Japanese society under Allied occupation.

The unification of China

By 1950 Mao Zedong had succeeded in unifying China, partly by demonstrating that the People's Liberation Army (PLA) was no warlord army. Soldiers, workers, the Party hierarchy (cadres), and the government were united. Mao assured the people that China was no longer isolated: the Sino–Soviet Treaty (1950) guaranteed their membership of an international socialist brotherhood. He promised land reform and development plans, and protection for China's frontiers. His first move was to invade Tibet in the winter of 1950–51 to recover what China considered a historic province.

War in Korea

North Korea invaded South Korea in 1950. This provoked a major United Nations response and an army from 16 nations, spearheaded by the Americans, was sent to Korea to resist the invaders. UN forces attacked across the 38th Parallel dividing North from South, and a few reached the border with China on the Yalu River. At this point the People's Liberation Army entered the war and forced a UN retreat. A static war ensued, with both sides digging in. An armistice was agreed at Panmunjom in 1953 and five years later the PLA left Korea, although a UN presence remained. After the war, North Korea remained a Stalinist state, while the South began to rebuild its shattered economy. Heavy industry and infrastructure, as well as electronics and consumer industries, were all constructed from scratch as Korea, like Japan, used the opportunity of war to build a new prosperity.

Maoist China

In the 1950s and 1960s, Mao Zedong attempted to forge a Chinese version of Marxism, based on a drive toward establishing economic modernization, especially in the chaotic "Great Leap Forward" of 1958–60, Mao's plan to increase agricultural and

38th Parallel

Line of latitude that divides North and South Korea. The 38th Parallel was first established to separate Soviet and U.S. occupation zones after Japan's defeat in 1945.

Curriculum Context

Students should focus on the causes and international and local consequences of major Cold War crises, such as the Korean War.

China and Taiwan

In 1954, gunners from the Chinese PLA shelled the two small islands of Quemoy and Matsu, which were claimed by the Nationalist government based in Taiwan. PLA forces landed on other Nationalist islands and in 1958 resumed the shelling of Quemoy. The United States mobilized a massive fleet in the Taiwan Straits in support of Jiang Jieshi, who still claimed to be the legitimate ruler of the whole of mainland China. In 1962 PLA forces attempted to push across the Indian border and were poised to enter Assam. After brief fighting against ill-prepared Indian troops, the Chinese withdrew. Along the Ussuri River Chinese patrols clashed with Soviet troops in 1969.

Curriculum Context

Students of China should consider both the benefits and the costs of policies under Mao Zedong, including the Great Leap Forward and the Cultural Revolution.

industrial production. This involved the collectivization of agriculture and forcing over 100 million people into projects such as the construction of irrigation systems. From the mid-1960s he fomented "permanent revolution" by encouraging the youthful Red Guards to challenge all forms of authority, especially in education, administration, industry, and the Party itself, and to send many intellectuals to work on communes. This lead to a wave of violence against intellectuals and others that severely damaged China's economy. China was almost totally cut off from the outside world until after Mao's death in 1976.

East Asian independence

Independence and unity arrived slowly for many east Asian nations. The Philippines became an independent republic in 1946; Burma in 1948; after the partition of India in 1947, East Pakistan became Bangladesh in 1971. But the former French Indo-Chinese colonies of Laos, Cambodia, and Vietnam became embroiled in the longest war of the century. During World War II the French had accepted Japanese domination of the area; only the Communist Vietminh forces led by Ho Chi Minh resisted, and declared independence in 1945. The return of the French led to a long guerrilla war in which

Vietminh

North Vietnamese organization, lead by Ho Chi Minh (founder of the Vietnamese nationalist movement) to drive the French out of their Indo-China colony.

the French initially drove the Vietminh from the major
cities, but in 1953–54 the Vietminh general Giap won
a remarkable and decisive victory over the French at
Dien Bien Phu.

Communist support for insurgents

Maoist China was the chief supporter of the insurgents
in Indo-China, and also of the Communists in Malaya
who inspired a long guerrilla campaign against the
British; eventually independence was achieved by
the anti-Communist, Malay-led nationalists in 1957.
Indonesia, which claimed its independence after the
war and won Dutch acceptance of the fact in 1949 after
a bitter struggle, also suffered Communist, regionalist,
and Islamist activity. To a lesser extent, the Philippines
(where United States' influence was still paramount),
Burma, and Thailand also saw Communist movements.

Curriculum Context

An interesting aspect of
this period is why some
Asian countries achieved
independence through
constitutional devolution
of power and others after
armed revolution.

Central and South Asia

In the latter half of the 20th century India and other central and south Asian countries gained independence, Bangladesh and Pakistan were created, and Tibet came under Chinese control.

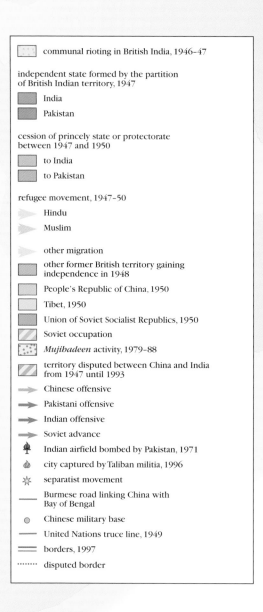

communal rioting in British India, 1946–47

independent state formed by the partition of British Indian territory, 1947

India

Pakistan

cession of princely state or protectorate between 1947 and 1950

to India

to Pakistan

refugee movement, 1947–50

Hindu

Muslim

other migration

other former British territory gaining independence in 1948

People's Republic of China, 1950

Tibet, 1950

Union of Soviet Socialist Republics, 1950

Soviet occupation

Mujihadeen activity, 1979–88

territory disputed between China and India from 1947 until 1993

Chinese offensive

Pakistani offensive

Indian offensive

Soviet advance

Indian airfield bombed by Pakistan, 1971

city captured by Taliban militia, 1996

separatist movement

Burmese road linking China with Bay of Bengal

Chinese military base

United Nations truce line, 1949

borders, 1997

disputed border

Kashi
(Kashgar)
☆ Uighur
separatists

Shache
(Yarkand)

PEOPLE'S REPUBLIC
OF CHINA

Khotan

TAJIKISTAN
to Soviet Union
1991 independent

K U N L U N   M T S

1962

anbu

1950

Han Chinese

5 million

luduz,
-Khumri

Tibetan Plateau

Northern Areas
part of Jammu and
Kashmir to 1947

Kashmiri
separatists

Aksai Chin region,
occupied by China
from 1962

Xizang
(Tibet)
1950 to China,
1965 nominally autonomous

1950

Peshawar
Islamabad

Srinagar

bad
ni

Rawalpindi

Jammu and
Kashmir
1947 to India

Thaga La

Jammu

1971

☆ Tibetan
separatists

1962

1962

Dukou

Dongchuan

Gujranwala

Pathankot
Lahore
1965
1971
Faisalabad

Dharamsala

Amritsar
1965
Faridkot Ambala

under Indian
influence until 1971

Lhasa

Kunming
Xiaguan

Multan
1971

Sikh separatists
from 1980

Delhi
Meerut

Sikkim
Indian protectorate
1974 to India

Brahmaputra

1962

Nagaland
separatists

Myitkyina

Chindwin

Sutlej

5.8 million
4.1 million
New Delhi

Bareilly

Kathmandu

NEPAL

BHUTAN
Thimphu

Guwahati

Bhamo

VIETN

MYANMAR
Burma until 1989
1948 independent

Namtu
Lashio

Faisalabad

Thar Desert

Bikaner

Agra

Lucknow

Ganges

Ayodhya

Ghaghara

10 million

Farakka dam

1971

0.3 million

1971

Jodhpur

Pokaran
Nuclear Test center

Jaipur

Gwalior

Yamuna

Allahabad

Patna

1.0 million
3.3 million

Dhaka

1971

Agartala

Monywa

Irrawaddy

Mandalay

Mon Tai
army

LAO

Rajasthan
1949 to India
0.7 million
1.2 million

Kota

Varanasi
(Benares)

Ranchi

Chandannagar
to France,
1954 to India

Calcutta

Khulna

Chittagong

Taunggyi

Bhopal

Narmada
Jabalpur

BANGLADESH
East Pakistan until 1971
1947 to Pakistan,
1971 independent

Karenni
separatists

tch

Ahmadabad

Indore

West Bengal

Magwe

Sittwe

THAILAND

Rajkot

Vadodara
(Baroda)

Nagpur

Mahanadi

Irrawaddy

Pegu

Diu
to Portugal,
2 to India

Daman
to Portugal,
1962 to India

Surat

Nasik

Aurangabad

INDIA
1947 independent

DECCAN

Godavari

Bay of
Bengal

Rangoon

Bassein

Moulmein

Karen
separatists

Bombay
(Mumbai)

Poone

Sholapur

Hyderabad
1949 to India

Hyderabad

Vishakhapatnam

Tavoy

Goa
to Portugal,
1962 to India

Krishna

Vijayawada

Yanam
to France,
1954 to India

Great Coco
Island

Mergui

Andaman Islands
to Britain,
1947 to India

Victoria Point

Mysore
1947 to India

Sriharikota Island
rocket launch site

Bangalore

Vellore

Madras
(Chennai)

Port Blair

Mysore

Kaveri

Pondicherry
to France,
1954 to India

Nicobar Islands
to Britain,
1947 to India

Laccadive Islands
to Britain,
1947 to India

Mahé
to France,
1954 to India

Coimbatore

Madurai

Karikal
to France,
1954 to India

0.8 million Tamils

Jaffna

Tamil Tigers
from 1985

Thumba
Vikram Sarabhai
Space center

Trincomalee

SRI LANKA
Ceylon until 1972
1948 independent

Colombo

Kandy

MALDIVES
1965 independent

Central and South Asia

India played an important part in the Allied war effort in 1939–45 and expectations of political change were high. However, the main parties, the Congress Party led by Mahatma Gandhi and Jawaharlal Nehru, and Mohammed Jinnah's Muslim League, were hostile to one another.

Curriculum Context

Important aspects of Indian nationalism are its impact on other movements in Asia and the partition of the subcontinent into India and Pakistan.

By 1945 the British government was already committed to Indian independence and sent representatives to attempt to resolve the differences between the Congress Party and the League. However, enmity between Muslims and Hindus caused rioting in the Indian cities of Calcutta and Delhi, and the British government decided on a rapid withdrawal. Lord Louis Mountbatten was charged with this task as violence spread across the entire Ganges valley. Consequently, two independent republics—a divided, predominantly Muslim Pakistan as well as India itself—were carved out of the subcontinent in 1947. Partition brought renewed civil conflict plus mass migration as millions of Muslims moved from India to East and West Pakistan and Hindus and Sikhs made their way to India. Appalled by the suffering, Mahatma Gandhi began a religious fast, only to be assassinated by a Hindu.

The formation of Bangladesh

The two republics continued to dispute Kashmir, and a war in 1948–49 led to a UN truce line across Kashmir. The truce lasted until 1965, when troops from both sides crossed the ceasefire line. Hostilities flared again in 1971, after Bangla Desh guerrillas in East Pakistan clashed with troops sent from West Pakistan by president Yahya Khan. Ten million refugees crossed from East Pakistan into India, imposing enormous strain on West Bengal. In December 1971, India invaded East Pakistan in support of the guerrillas and defeated the Pakistani army. The region gained its independence as Bangladesh. The country's first prime minister, Sheikh Mujibur, who nationalized the jute, tea, and textile industries, was assassinated, as was president Zia Rahman.

Progress and change in India

As a secular state India tried to change long-established customs through parliamentary legislation. The minimum age for women to marry was raised and the right of divorce was granted; discrimination against *harijans* (untouchables) was outlawed. When Congress Party leader Indira Gandhi became prime minister in 1966, her watchword was *Garibi Hatao* ("reduce poverty"). She invested heavily in industry,

Curriculum Context

Students should study the connections between the rise of independence movements in southeast Asia and social transformations such as demographic changes and urbanization.

Indira Gandhi's assassination by Sikh bodyguards was an act of revenge for her army's killing of hundreds of Sikhs during a raid on the Sikh Golden Temple at Amritsar a few months before.

food-grain production, and family planning, including compulsory sterilization. She made many enemies and was assassinated in 1984 by her own Sikh bodyguard.

By this time India was an industrial and military power. It had fought China in the Himalayas, acquired nuclear military technology in 1974, and launched a satellite into orbit. India had built up an aerospace industry and a navy that included a potent carrier fleet. During the 1990s India's economy was steadily liberalized and measures of positive discrimination were taken in favor of people of lower castes and minorities. Prime minister Rajiv Gandhi was assassinated in 1991, and riots continued to blight cities such as Bombay as Hindu fundamentalism began to challenge the constitutional assumptions of the state.

Liberalized

In terms of economics, this means a relaxation of previous government restrictions in order to allow market forces to regulate the relations between economic agents.

Pakistan

In Pakistan in the 1960s, Zulfikar Ali Bhutto tried to initiate a program of nationalization (or "Islamic socialism") but his ruthless approach led to his execution by President Zia ul-Haq, who later died in an air crash. Bhutto's daughter, Benazir, then began a stormy political career and was prime minister in the early 1990s. From independence Pakistan had powerful military forces and in the 1990s it was suspected to have nuclear weapons comparable with India's Prithvi missiles. It was threatened by endemic corruption and Islamized state and society, especially after the Soviet invasion of Afghanistan in 1979 caused a huge influx of refugees.

Curriculum Context

World War II and postwar global politics had an impact on the rise of mass nationalist movements in southeast Asia.

Burma and Sri Lanka

Burma (now the Union of Myanmar) experienced little of the democracy promised after General Aung San led it to independence in 1948. His daughter, Aung San Suu Kyi, opposed military rule but was held under house arrest through much of the 1990s. Burma enjoyed Chinese support in return for bases at Coco

The Chinese in Tibet

Tibet, occupied by the People's Republic of China in 1950, experienced military rule after the failure of the Lhasa rebellion and the flight of the Dalai Lama to India in 1959. The Chinese declared the Dalai Lama a traitor and when his successor, the Panchen Lama, died in 1989, installed a puppet ruler; mass immigration of Han Chinese to the region threatened to swamp the indigenous population.

Island and Victoria Point. Sri Lanka, also independent in 1948, was racked by civil war between the minority Tamils and the Sinhalese from 1983. The Tamil Tigers attempted to establish an independent state in the north of the island and captured Jaffna in 1991. The government retook the city in 1996 as Tamil bomb squads resorted to terrorism.

Afghanistan

Afghanistan tried to retain its independence during the Cold War, but in 1973 its constitutional monarchy was ousted and the Communists became stronger. In 1979 the government sought Soviet assistance against the Muslim Mujihadeen guerrillas. Soviet occupation forces suffered heavy losses against the guerrillas and finally withdrew after the peace settlement negotiated with Afghan president Najibullah in 1988. The Soviet withdrawal paved the way for a bitter civil war, and in 1996 the Taliban militia, an extreme fundamentalist Islamist group, captured Kabul. After the Taliban supported the terrorist network that carried out the September 11, 2001, terrorist attacks in the United States, U.S. military forces invaded the country and removed the Taliban from power. Afghanistan adopted a presidential form of government in 2004.

Dramatic changes in central Asia followed the breakup of the Soviet Union in 1991, as a series of former Soviet republics in the Caucasus and along the Iranian and Chinese frontiers declared themselves independent.

Tamil Tigers

Terrorist organization in Sri Lanka that seeks to establish an independent Tamil state and relies on guerrilla tactics, such as targeting key government and military personnel.

Curriculum Context

It is important to understand why terrorist movements have proliferated and the extent of their impact on politics and society in various countries.

The Rise of the Pacific Rim

The rapid industrialization of Asian countries from the 1970s created a new global focus for manufacture, notably high technology and investment.

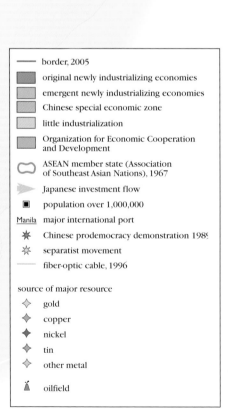

Legend

— border, 2005

■ original newly industrializing economies

■ emergent newly industrializing economies

■ Chinese special economic zone

■ little industrialization

■ Organization for Economic Cooperation and Development

◖ ASEAN member state (Association of Southeast Asian Nations), 1967

▷ Japanese investment flow

■ population over 1,000,000

<u>Manila</u> major international port

✳ Chinese prodemocracy demonstration 1989

✸ separatist movement

— fiber-optic cable, 1996

source of major resource

◇ gold

◈ copper

◆ nickel

◈ tin

◇ other metal

⚱ oilfield

Map labels

Yumen • Jiayugu

CHINA

La

BHUTAN

NEPAL

BANGLADESH

INDIA

Kun

Irrawaddy

Mandalay

MYANMAR
Burma until 1989,
1997 joined ASEAN

Vientian

Rangoon

THA

Ban

Pinang

Medan

Putrajaya

Padang

Pale

Sum

I N D I A
O C E A

The Rise of the Pacific Rim

The balance of world power was dramatically altered by the rise of the Asian economies in the last quarter of the 20th century, which was driven by the region's plentiful supplies of cheap labor able to take on work of a highly technical nature.

Infrastructure projects, heavy industry, textiles, and high technology were developed in parallel to allow these countries—many of them, such as South Korea and China, devastated by political turmoil in mid-century—to emerge from poverty to compete on the world stage within a few decades.

Japanese trade and investment

The economic power driving this development was that of Japan, which trebled its investments in many of the east and southeast Asian countries after 1985, when a revaluation of the Yen made home-produced goods uncompetitive. By the late 1990s, the east and southeast Asian countries had overtaken the United States as Japan's main trading partner, with Malaysia, Hong Kong, Taiwan, and, increasingly, China, as the main beneficiaries.

Revaluation

Alteration of the relative value of a currency, based on criteria such as wage rates or the international price of gold, causing a rise in the price of goods or products.

Tiger economies

The tiger, or dragon, economies of Asia—South Korea, Hong Kong, Taiwan, and Singapore—grew up alongside Japan. These newly industrializing economies (NIEs) had a number of characteristics in common. None had significant raw materials, so all had to export in order to grow. From the 1950s all nurtured their industries by government protection and all turned to export-oriented small light industries in the 1960s and 1970s. Like Japan, they had lost the advantage of low labor costs by the mid 1990s, and moved to invest in their neighbors with reserves of even cheaper labor, notably China.

The Vietnamese opportunity

As the region developed, new countries opened up for development. Japan and Korea competed for a position in the Vietnam economy, especially after relations between Vietnam and the United States were normalized in 1995. Vietnam's transport and energy infrastructure was particularly weak following the destruction caused by the war that ended in 1975.

Korean trading

By the 1980s South Korea had shifted its manufacturing base toward transportation, high technology, and heavy industry, and growth continued at a high rate. South Korean firms slowly opened trading links with the Communist regime in North Korea, but relationships between the two countries remained tense even after the death in 1994 of Kim Il Sung, ruler of North Korea since its foundation.

Made by Taiwan

The foundations for Taiwan's economy were laid by Jiang Ching-kuo, the son of Chinese Nationalist leader Jiang Jieshi, from the late 1970s. He developed shipbuilding, petrochemicals, and electronic industries, especially computers. By the mid-1990s this small island, remarkably, had the eighth largest trading power in the world. Mainland China, however, regarded Taiwan as a part of the People's Republic; Taiwan's democratic elections in 1987, and the election in 1996 of a leader more committed to an independent Taiwanese future, exacerbated tensions between the two.

Tigers diversify

Hong Kong, China's small offshore island leased to Britain until 1997, moved toward trade and banking but retained its textile and other labor-intensive industries. Singapore, by contrast, pursued high-technology manufacture in conjunction with finance and business services.

High technology

Most advanced technology currently available, based on intensive research and development and specialized manufacture, often referring to electronics or optics.

Curriculum Context

Students should assess the impact of the continuing growth of mass consumption of commodities and resources since World War II on the economies of Asia.

The transformation of China

In 1975, China had little or no foreign investment, no foreign loans, and little direct trade with non-Communist states other than Japan. In 1978, vice-premier Deng Xiaoping embarked on economic and educational reforms, aiming to replace Mao Zedong's class struggle with the goal of economic modernization. Political reform, however, was not pursued and a prodemocracy movement that arose in the wake of economic reform was crushed in 1989. Despite worldwide condemnation of China's human rights record, China actively sought investment, trade, and technology from overseas. South Korea located plant and machinery in China's special economic zones; but the tiger economies that did most in China were those with the strongest political or ethnic ties with the country—notably Singapore and Taiwan (even though trade between Taiwan and mainland China was officially illegal).

From 1984 Hong Kong, many of whose inhabitants came from Guangdong province, increasingly shifted its production to nearby Chinese provinces to take advantage of lower labor costs. The return of Hong Kong to Chinese control in 1997 was a big step toward further integration of the two economies.

New players in the region

Japan retained its status as economic superpower thanks to its technological superiority, even though its growth was slowing in the 1990s while other Asian countries beside China were industrializing fast. Thailand, Malaysia, and Indonesia—which has large reserves of oil and gas to finance the growth of heavy industries such as petrochemicals, shipbuilding, and steel—were growing. The Philippines, too, opted in the mid-1990s for policies modeled on the successes of other economies of the region.

Special economic zone

Region with different economic rules from the rest of a country, set up to generate investment, exports, employment, and development of infrastructure.

Curriculum Context

Students should study the causes and consequences of the world's shift from bipolar to multipolar centers of economic and political power.

Outsiders in Asia

A few countries did not form part of the "Asian miracle": notably Cambodia and Myanmar (formerly Burma), where oppressive regimes deterred foreign investment, and Laos, which had poor infrastructure. Nevertheless the cheap pools of labor in these countries were expected to prove attractive to investors as wages elsewhere began to rise.

Political changes

Politically, despite the intrusion of global market forces, the region saw the survival of Communism as the dominant ideology in China, Vietnam, North Korea, and among some Filipino insurgents. Hong Kong witnessed belated democratic development after 1992 in an effort to protect the rights of its inhabitants after it was reincorporated into China in 1997.

New Pacific Rim alliances

Profound changes in attitude toward the rising Asian economies occurred among the older democracies—Canada, Australia, and New Zealand, as well as the United States—of the Pacific Rim. Initially seeing themselves as investors and suppliers to the new economies, they rapidly became consumers of Asian goods. By the 1980s the Commonwealth countries had moved away from historic ties with Britain and accepted the arrival of Asian-owned companies, and radically changed their immigration laws to permit the settlement of Asian immigrants.

Asian miracle

Change of certain South Asian countries from technologically backward, poor economies to modern, affluent economies following external investment and internal innovation.

Curriculum Context

It is important to understand how countries of the Pacific Rim such as South Korea or Singapore have achieved economic growth in recent decades.

The Middle East and North Africa

The decline of colonialism in the Middle
East and North Africa was a consequence
of a rise in nationalism and also reflected
a European intention to ensure access to
the great oil resources of the region.

SPAIN

Spanish Morocco
Gibraltar to Britain
Nov 1942
Tangier • Ceuta
Melilla
Oran •
Algiers
Bizerte
Nov 1942
1921–26
Tunis
Sousse
Malta to Britain
Casablanca • Fedala Fez
1945 1942–03
Tunisia
Safi
French Morocco
Marrakech
Bechar
Laghouat
Touggourt
Tozeur Gabes
Tripoli
1942–43
Algeria
Tripolitania
1934 united with Cyrenaica,
1947 under British administration
Tindouf
Libya
1912–32 Italian conquest, then became
Italian colony
In Salah
Fezzan
1939 united with Cyrenaica
and Tripolitania,
1947 under French administration
Ghat
Murzuq •
SAHARA DE

Med

G

Beng

C
193
T
1947
ad

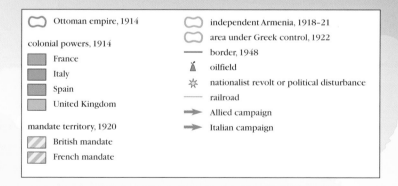

	Ottoman empire, 1914		independent Armenia, 1918–21
			area under Greek control, 1922
colonial powers, 1914			border, 1948
	France		oilfield
	Italy		nationalist revolt or political disturbance
	Spain		railroad
	United Kingdom		Allied campaign
mandate territory, 1920			Italian campaign
	British mandate		
	French mandate		

1918–23 Istanbul

Ankara 1918–23
TURKEY
Ottoman empire until 1923

Kars
site of massacre, 1915

Caspian
Sea

Tabriz
1931–32, 1935–36,
1943–44
Lake
Urmia
Tehran

Izmir
1918–23
Konya 1918–23
1918–23
Adana
Ufra 1933
1937–39
1920–21
Aleppo

Mosul
1919, 1922–27,
1930–31
Kirkuk

Hamadan

IRAN
Persia until 1935,
1941–42 Allied occupation

Athens
1918–23

Crete

Latakia 1989
Nicosia
Cyprus
Homs
SYRIA 1920–41 French mandate,
1946 independent
Beirut 1936, 1943
LEBANON
1920–41 French mandate,
1946 independent
Damascus
PALESTINE
1920–48 British mandate
Tel Aviv
Amman
Jerusalem
1920, 1936–39
1925–27,
1937–39
1929
Aug–Oct 1918

1920
Baghdad

1920, 1935
1936, 1941
IRAQ
1920–32 British mandate,
1932 independent
Habbiniyah
Oct 1914–Nov 1918
An Najaf

Isfahan

Kerman

Ranean Sea

Tobruk
1942
Alexandria
1919
Suez
Canal
Cairo Suez
Aqaba
JORDAN
1920–46 British mandate,
Transjordan until independent 1946

Shaiba
Basra
Abadan
Kuwait
Kuwait

Shiraz

Persian Gulf

Bandar Abbas

EGYPT
1914 British protectorate,
1922 independent

El Kharga

Aswan

1916
Medina
Hejaz
1916 independent,
1926 to Nejd

SAUDI ARABIA
1916–26 Nejd,
1926–32 Hejaz and Nejd

Riyadh

Al Manamah Bahrain
Qatar
Doha Abu Dhabi

Trucial Oman

Muscat

Oman

Wadi Halfa

Jiddah
Mecca

Asir
1917 independent,
1920 to Nejd

Red Sea

Port Sudan
Suakin

Anglo-Egyptian
Sudan

Omdurman
Khartoum

Kassala

Sennar

El Obeid

Jizan
Eritrea
1941 under British
administration
Asmera
Massawa
Adowa
Jan–Sep 1941
Oct 1935–May 1936
Gondar
1941
Apr 1941
Blue Nile
White Nile
Addis Ababa
ETHIOPIA
1936–41 to Italy,
1941 independence restored

YEMEN
1919 independent
Sana

Mukalla
Hadramaut
(East Aden
Protectorate)

Socotra

West Aden
Protectorate
Aden

French
Somaliland
Djibouti

Berbera
British Somaliland

INDIAN
OCEAN

Harar
Mar–Apr 1941

Walwal
Apr–May 1936
Shebelle

Italian Somaliland
Italian protectorate until 1941,
1941 under British administration

The Middle East and North Africa

After World War I (1914–18), African nations that had been part of the German or Ottoman empires were redistributed among Allies under the Covenant of the League of Nations (1918). The covenant pledged to help underdeveloped peoples cope with the "strenuous conditions of the modern world" before they gained full independence.

Mandate

Formal commission granted by the League of Nations authorizing a member nation to administer the affairs of another.

Some ex-colonies were scheduled for rapid independence: on this understanding Britain was awarded a mandate over Palestine, Iraq (formerly Mesopotamia), and Transjordan; France gained Syria and Lebanon. Independence was delayed for less advanced areas in the region: these included Ruanda–Urundi, awarded to Belgium, and the Cameroons and Togoland, shared by Britain and France.

Palestine and Israel

The British government favored the establishment of a national home for the Jews in Palestine. This conflicted with an earlier promise to the Arabs that their new lands would include Palestine, where the population was 90 percent Muslim. Jewish immigration to the area grew substantially in the 1930s, when the British first proposed the division of Palestine into separate Jewish and Arab states. After World War II, with the world horrified by the Holocaust and the Jews and Arabs in Palestine engaged in civil war, the United Nations supported partition and approved the state of Israel, which came into being in 1948.

Curriculum Context

Students of the Middle East and North Africa should understand how collapse of the German and Ottoman empires and the creation of new states affected international relations in the Middle East.

Iran and Lebanon

In 1932 Britain permitted the Saudi kingdom to emerge and its mandate in Iraq ended in 1932, although it retained the right to protect oil and military interests. A native Pahlavi dynasty seized control of Persia in 1925, renaming it Iran in 1935. The shah's ties with Nazi Germany led the Allies to occupy the country in 1941; the shah was forced to abdicate and his son installed in his place. The market for Middle Eastern oil grew in the interwar years, but the oilfields were not fully developed until the 1950s. French rule in Syria and Lebanon was benevolent, but was compromised by the fall of France in 1940; both countries were occupied during the war by French and British troops, and their independent status was recognized in 1946.

Egypt and the Sudan

The British confirmed Egyptian independence in 1922. British policy toward Egypt and the Sudan involved little or no settlement from Britain. The British saw Egypt as a major source of cotton, and encouraged Egyptian financial institutions to support local industry and cotton-related projects in the Sudan. By 1939 Egypt was approaching self-sufficiency in a range of manufactured goods; production rose further during the war years.

Britain had maintained the right to use Egypt's facilities in times of war, to defend the Suez Canal, and to maintain the Anglo-Egyptian condominium in the Sudan. The British in Egypt and Italians in Libya began a conflict in 1940 which drew in the German army the following year; by 1943 all countries along the entire North Africa coastline were involved.

Curriculum Context

An important aspect of the World War I settlement is how it contributed to the rise of both pan-Arabism and nationalist struggles for independence in the Middle East.

Condominium
Joint sovereignty or ownership of the same region.

Events in Ethiopia

Ethiopia had retained its independence from colonial rule since defeating the Italians in 1896, and from 1935 was ruled by Haile Selassie (formerly Ras Tafari), who faced an invasion from Italy's fascist dictator Mussolini. After using mustard gas on the Ethiopians, the Italians took Addis Ababa in 1936; a resistance movement continued to harry the Italians until World War II, when the British invaded and drove the Italians out once more, restoring Haile Selassie in 1941 and making Ethiopia the first African country to be liberated. Britain now took over the adminstration of the former Italian colonies of Eritrea and Somaliland.

Arab–Israeli Conflict

From 1948 the new state of
Israel attracted thousands of
Jewish immigrants, while
more than a million
Palestinians became refugees
in their own land, resulting
in Arab–Israeli conflict.

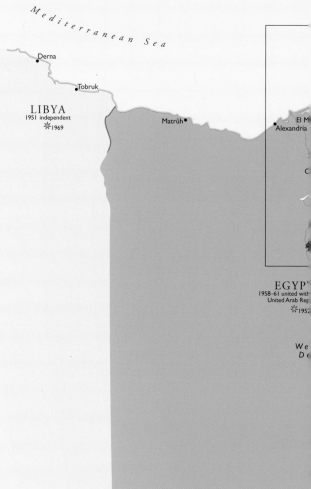

Mediterranean Sea

Derna

Tobruk

LIBYA
1951 independent
☆1969

Matrûh•

El M
Alexandria•

EGYP
1958–61 united with
United Arab Rep
☆195

W e
D e

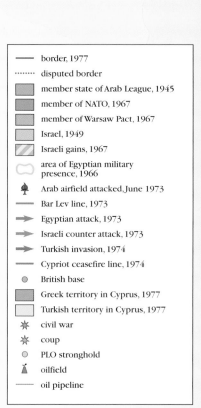

——	border, 1977
·······	disputed border
▨	member state of Arab League, 1945
▨	member of NATO, 1967
▨	member of Warsaw Pact, 1967
▢	Israel, 1949
▨	Israeli gains, 1967
◖◗	area of Egyptian military presence, 1966
♣	Arab airfield attacked, June 1973
—	Bar Lev line, 1973
➡	Egyptian attack, 1973
➡	Israeli counter attack, 1973
➡	Turkish invasion, 1974
—	Cypriot ceasefire line, 1974
◉	British base
▨	Greek territory in Cyprus, 1977
▢	Turkish territory in Cyprus, 1977
✳	civil war
✳	coup
◉	PLO stronghold
⚑	oilfield
——	oil pipeline

Lake Van
Tabriz
Lake Urmia
Kurdish risings 1945–46, 1961–75
IRAN
Kerman
TURKEY
1960, 1971
Adana
Gaziantep
Dörtyol
Aleppo
SYRIA
1946 independent, 1958–61 united with Egypt as United Arab Republic
1949, 1961, 1963, 1966, 1970
Euphrates
Latakia
Hamah
Homs
Mosul
Arbil
Kirkuk
Diyala
Tigris
Bahr al Tharthar
Baghdad
IRAQ
1958, 1963, 1968
Al Hillah
An Najaf
Basra
KUWAIT
1961 independent
neutral zone
Nicosia
1955–77
Dhekelia
Akrotiri
Tripoli
1946 independent
LEBANON
1975–89
Beirut
Sidon
Dumeir
Damascus
GOLAN HEIGHTS
Syrian Desert
Haifa
WEST BANK
Tel Aviv–Jaffa
ISRAEL
1948 independent
Mafraq
Amman
Jerusalem
Hebron
Gaza
Dead Sea
Karak
JORDAN
1946 independent
1970
Port Said
El Arish
Jebel Libni
Abu Sueir
Bir Gifgafa
Bir Thamada
Suez
Battle of Chinese Farm, 1973
Aqaba
Sudr
Abu Rudeis
Ras Gharib
Sharm el Sheikh
SAUDI ARABIA
Eastern Desert
Hurghada
Red Sea
Luxor
Aswan
Aswan High Dam completed 1970
Lake Nasser
Ras Banas
area disputed from 1958
SUDAN
1956 independent
1962–69
1958, 1969
Mecca
LEBANON
Tyre
SYRIA
Mediterranean Sea
from Cyprus
from Malta
Zefat
Haifa
Jordan
WEST BANK
Nablus
Tel Aviv–Jaffa
Amman
Jerusalem
Jericho
Bethlehem
GAZA STRIP
Gaza
Hebron
Dead Sea
Port Said
El Arish
Beersheba
El Mansura
El Qantara
Suez Canal
Romani
Imailia
Bir Hasana
Bir Gifgafa
Negev
JORDAN
EGYPT
Cairo
Mitla Pass
Oct 1956
El Kuntilla
Suez
Sudr
El Thamad
Eilat
Aqaba
SINAI
Abu Zenima
SAUDI ARABIA
Dahab
Gulf of Aqaba
Nov 1956
El Tur
Sharm el Sheikh
border, 1956
Israel, 1948
Israeli gains, 1948–49
Arab refugee camp, 1948
Israeli airborne attack, 1956
Israeli campaign, 1956
Anglo-French airborne and sea landing, 5–6 Nov 1956
0 200 km
0 150 mi

Arab–Israeli Conflict

Only a few hours after the proclamation of the independent state of Israel on May 14, 1948, the armies of Syria, Jordan, Egypt, and Iraq invaded, expecting to crush the Jewish state and establish an Arab Palestine. Israel drew on reserves of experienced soldiers from around the world, defeated the Arabs, and conquered territory as far as West Jerusalem.

Curriculum Context

Students should understand how international conditions affected the creation of Israel.

Defeat led to a nationalist revolt in Egypt in 1952, when the British-sponsored ruling family was expelled and a republic formed. Colonel Nasser, president from 1954, relied on U.S. dollars to build the massive Aswan Dam, regarded as essential for Egypt's economic and industrial development. When the United States withdrew as a response to Nasser's increasingly anti-western foreign policy, he nationalized the Suez Canal, long seen as a strategic key to the east by Britain and France. Israel's support was secured and Israeli forces invaded Sinai in October 1956, followed by Anglo-French troops. A United Nations force was sent in; Nasser blocked the canal with sunken ships.

The Six-Day War

There followed increased superpower involvement in the region: Arab states turned to the Soviet Union for weaponry while the United States became Israel's arsenal. Nasser believed that Egypt and Syria (united as the United Arab Republic in 1958–61), would defeat Israel. With an alliance of Arab states he provoked a crisis by closing the Gulf of Aqaba. Israel, however, launched a pre-emptive strike, destroying most Egyptian combat aircraft in June 1967; Syria and Jordan suffered similar losses. When a ceasefire was agreed six days later, Israeli forces had occupied Gaza and the entire Sinai east of Suez, Jordan surrendered East Jerusalem, Bethlehem, and Hebron, and Syria lost the Golan Heights, an area dominating the north of Israel.

United Arab Republic

Arab-Muslim union formed by Egypt and Syria, which ceased to exist when Syria left the union in September 1961. Egypt continued to use the name for itself until 1971.

The Palestinian Liberation Organization

The United Nations passed resolutions requiring Israel to evacuate the occupied territories and confirming Palestinian rights to self-determination within Israel, where the Palestinians were treated as second-class citizens and many lived in refugee camps. The Palestinian Liberation Organization (PLO) was founded in 1964. By the early 1970s it had won, through terrorist tactics and moral pressure, a powerful voice in the region. Seeming to endanger the fragile stability of Jordan, the PLO was evicted from the kingdom in 1970 and settled in Lebanon.

The Yom Kippur War

In October 1973 Egypt's new president Anwar Sadat broke into Israeli-held territory without warning on the Jewish Day of Atonement (Yom Kippur). The Israelis concentrated on holding the Golan Heights against Syrian tanks, but three weeks later Israel had defeated both attacks while the two superpowers refused to intervene actively to support the protagonists.

Oil crisis of 1973

In response to the United States' supply of military materiel to the Israelis, Saudi Arabia (the leading member of the Organization of Petroleum Exporting Countries, OPEC) imposed oil sanctions on the west. However, the main oil-producing states were reluctant to give military support to the anti-Israeli effort, and tensions developed between Saudi Arabia and Egypt. Syria, Iraq, and Libya, other important oil producers, were also run by anti-American regimes.

First steps toward peace

Following the Yom Kippur War, Menachem Begin became prime minister of Israel and realized that Sadat was interested in reducing Arab–Israeli tensions. Begin invited Sadat to Jerusalem to initiate a peace process that was formalized in 1979.

Sanctions

Sanctions imposed by OPEC in the 1970s involved the restriction of OPEC exports, which caused a sharp price rise.

Curriculum Context

An important aspect of the oil crisis in the early 1970s was the way its aftermath revealed the extent and complexity of global economic interdependence.

The Middle East Since 1977

Late 20th-century territorial wars in the Middle East raged between Israel and neighbors over Palestine in the west, and between Iran, Iraq, and Kuwait over religion and oil in the east.

TURKEY

Incirlik • Gaziantep
Dörtyol

• Aleppo

CYPRUS   Latakia •   • Hamah
Nicosia • Famagusta   • Homs
from 1964
Akrotiri   from 1978
                Beirut   • Damascus
to Algeria and Tunisia   from 1974
from eastern Europe   Haifa • GOLAN HEIGHTS
                         ISRAEL
                Tel Aviv–Jaffa • WEST BANK
                Jerusalem • Jericho
                GAZA • Amman
                STRIP Dead
Alexandria •   Port Said •   Sea
                         JORDAN
                1975–79
            Cairo • • Suez   • Aqaba
EGYPT   • Sudr SINAI
        Ras Gharib • Abu
                Rudeis   Tabuk

Eastern Desert

Western
Desert

• Aswan

Lake
Nasser

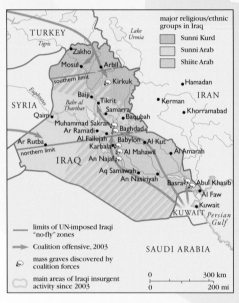

major religious/ethnic groups in Iraq

- Sunni Kurd
- Sunni Arab
- Shiite Arab

TURKEY   Lake Urmia
Tigris
        • Zakho
Mosul • • Arbil
        Kirkuk
southern limit
        • Hamadan
Baiji •   IRAN
SYRIA Tikrit • Kerman
Qaim • Samarra
    Bahr al   • Khorramabad
    Tharthar • Baqubah
Muhammad Sakran • Baghdad
Ar Ramadi •
Ar Rutba • Al Fallujah Babylon • Al Kut
northern limit Karbala • • Al Mahawil • Al Amarah
    IRAQ An Najaf
        Aq Samawah
            An Nasiriyah
                Basra • • Abul Khasib
                    • Al Faw
                • Kuwait
            KUWAIT Persian Gulf

——— limits of UN-imposed Iraqi "no-fly" zones

➤ Coalition offensive, 2003

↩ mass graves discovered by coalition forces

⬭ main areas of Iraqi insurgent activity since 2003

SAUDI ARABIA

0   300 km
0   200 mi

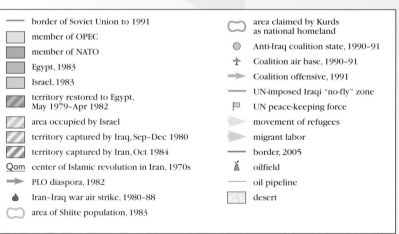

———	border of Soviet Union to 1991	⬭ area claimed by Kurds as national homeland
▢	member of OPEC	⬤ Anti-Iraq coalition state, 1990–91
▢	member of NATO	✟ Coalition air base, 1990–91
▢	Egypt, 1983	➤ Coalition offensive, 1991
▢	Israel, 1983	——— UN-imposed Iraqi "no-fly" zone
▨	territory restored to Egypt, May 1979–Apr 1982	⚑ UN peace-keeping force
▨	area occupied by Israel	▷ movement of refugees
▨	territory captured by Iraq, Sep–Dec 1980	▷ migrant labor
▨	territory captured by Iran, Oct 1984	——— border, 2005
Qom	center of Islamic revolution in Iran, 1970s	⚓ oilfield
➤	PLO diaspora, 1982	——— oil pipeline
🔥	Iran–Iraq war air strike, 1980–88	⬚ desert
⬭	area of Shiite population, 1983	

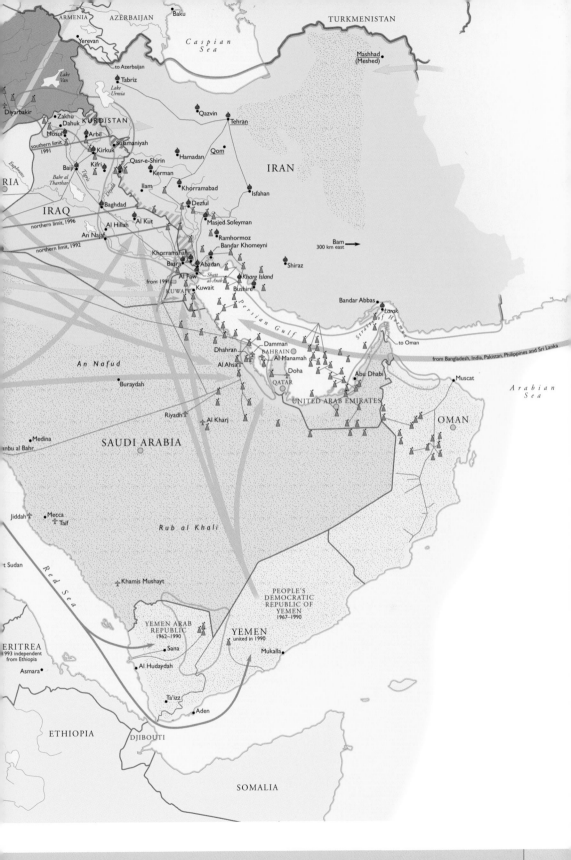

ARMENIA
AZERBAIJAN
Baku
TURKMENISTAN
Caspian Sea
Yerevan
to Azerbaijan
Mashhad (Meshed)
Lake Van
Tabriz
Lake Urmia
Diyarbakir
Qazvin
Zakhu
Dahuk
KURDISTAN
Tehran
Mosul
Arbil
Sulaimaniyah
southern limit 1991
Kirkuk
Hamadan
Qom
IRAN
Baiji
Kifri
Qasr-e-Shirin
Kerman
Bahr al Tharthar
Ilam
Khorramabad
Isfahan
Baghdad
Dezful
Al Hillah
Al Kut
Masjed Soleyman
northern limit, 1996
Ramhormoz
An Najaf
Bandar Khomeyni
Bam
300 km east
northern limit, 1992
Khorramshahr
Basra
Abadan
Kharg Island
Shiraz
Al Faw
Shatt al-Arab
from 1991
KUWAIT
Kuwait
Bushire
Bandar Abbas
Larak
Strait of Hormuz
to Oman
An Nafud
Dhahran
Damman
BAHRAIN
Al Manamah
from Bangladesh, India, Pakistan, Philippines and Sri Lanka
Al Ahsa
Doha
QATAR
Buraydah
Abu Dhabi
Muscat
Arabian Sea
UNITED ARAB EMIRATES
Riyadh
Al Kharj
OMAN
Medina
anbu al Bahr
SAUDI ARABIA
Jiddah
Mecca
Taif
Rub al Khali
t Sudan
Red Sea
Khamis Mushayt
PEOPLE'S DEMOCRATIC REPUBLIC OF YEMEN 1967–1990
ERITREA
1993 independent from Ethiopia
YEMEN ARAB REPUBLIC 1962–1990
YEMEN
united in 1990
Asmara
Sana
Mukalla
Al Hudaydah
Ta'izz
Aden
ETHIOPIA
DJIBOUTI
SOMALIA

The Middle East Since 1977

U.S. president Carter arranged meetings between Egypt's president Sadat and Israeli prime minister Begin at Camp David which led to a treaty in 1979 that recognized the state of Israel, promised autonomy to the Palestinians in Gaza and the West Bank, and returned the Sinai to Egypt.

The Palestine Liberation Organization (PLO) carried on fighting Israel through terrorist activities in Europe and from its Al Fatah bases in Lebanon, where civil war was raging between Christian Phalangist and Islamic forces. In 1978 Israel invaded and UN forces struggled to keep apart the Israeli, Syrian, and Christian armies. Sadat was assassinated by Islamic activists in 1981, but his successor Hosni Mubarak continued his policies. Trying to restore stability to the region, the United States brokered an agreement that the PLO leave Beirut, but Lebanon's civil war continued until Syria restored peace in the early 1990s. Hezbollah fighters funded by Iran still used Lebanese bases for raids on Israel.

Islamic rule in Iran

In Iran the pro-western shah was overthrown in 1979 and replaced by the Ayatollah Khomeini, president of a new theocratic republic. Khomeini cut diplomatic relations with Israel, welcomed PLO leader Yassir Arafat to Tehran, and defined the United States as the "main enemy of mankind." U.S. embassy staff were taken hostage; 52 stayed in captivity for over a year despite a trade embargo and an abortive rescue mission.

War with Iraq

Khomeini's resurgent Shiite Islam led Saddam Hussein, Ba'athist leader of predominantly Sunni Iraq, to invade Iran in 1980. War between the two states continued for eight years. By the ceasefire in 1988, almost a million had died and there was great damage to oil facilities

Curriculum Context

Students studying the Middle East should be able to explain why persistent conflict developed between Israel and both Arab Palestinians and neighboring states.

Theocratic

A theocratic government is one governed by religious leaders who rule as representatives of their god or deity using a legal system based on religious principles.

on both sides. In 1990, Saddam invaded the rich, pro-western emirate of Kuwait. The UN imposed sanctions and Saudi Arabia, fearing further Iraqi expansion, allowed its territory to be used as a base for an attack on Iraq. Despite Soviet support for Iraq, the UN agreed the use of force and war broke out in January 1991. Iraq tried to draw the entire region into the conflict by goading Israel with missile attacks, but the U.S.-led UN coalition (including Egypt and Syria) limited the scope of the conflict and won a quick victory.

Civil war in Iraq

After Kuwait had been liberated, civil war broke out in Iraq as Shiites in the south and the Kurds in the north both sought to secede. Saddam remained in power, destroying the Shiite powerbase and forcing two million Kurds to seek asylum in Iran and Turkey, before the UN stepped in to enforce no-fly zones and safe havens from Iraqi attack. Devastating sanctions were imposed, but Saddam rebuilt his military base, including chemical weapons (forbidden by the postwar agreement); he also gradually restored his authority over the Kurdish areas.

Israeli–Palestinian conflict continues

Meanwhile, the Camp David agreements on Palestinian rights failed: Jewish settlers moved into the West Bank and built virtual fortresses there. In 1987 Gaza and West Bank Palestinians began the *intifada* against Israelis. Eventually a peace process was agreed, with phased Israeli withdrawals and recognition of a Palestinian National Authority under Arafat, chairman of the PLO, initially only in Jericho but later intended to include Gaza and other areas. However, Israel faced a rightwing backlash and prime minister Rabin was murdered in 1995. Thereafter moves toward Palestinian self-rule advanced slowly amid mutual suspicion. U.S. president Barack Obama tried to revive the flagging peace process in 2009.

Secede
To withdraw or break away from membership of a political alliance.

Intifada
Uprising by Palestinian Arabs in the Gaza Strip and the West Bank against Israel.

Curriculum Context

Students should assess the progress that has been made since the 1970s in resolving conflict between Israel and neighboring states.

Decolonization and Nationalism in Africa

After World War II, African countries gradually became independent, but in places colonialism left a legacy of ethnic tensions that erupted into violence and civil war.

Spanish
Morocco
Rab

M

T

Western Sahara
1975 to Morocco
✳ 1957
✳ from 1975

Nouadhibou

Atar

MAURITANIA
1960 independent
1960; 1971–74;
1983

CAPE VERDE
1975 independent
✳ 1963–74
☞ 1983
Praia

Nouakchott

Senegal
St Louis
Kiffa
Dakar
SENEGAL
1960 independent
☞ 1971–74
1973

Kaédi
Kayes

GAMBIA
1965 independent
GUINEA-BISSAU
1974 independent
Banjul
Bissau
✳ 1959–74

Bamako

GUINEA
1958 independent
Conakry
Kankan
✳ 1991–2002

Sikasso

Bi

SIERRA LEONE
1961 independent
1997 coup
Freetown
Kenema

IVOR
COA
1960
independe

Monrovia
1985–95
2000–03

LIBERIA

Yamc

fr

prewar colonial powers

- Belgium
- France
- Italy
- Portugal
- Spain
- United Kingdom

- territory placed under UN trusteeship, 1946
- Federation of Rhodesia and Nyasaland, 1953–63
- border, 2005
- ✳ anti-colonial war
- ✳ civil war
- ✳ interstate war
- ☞ famine or humanitarian crisis
- area at risk of desertification, 1990s
- desert
- movement of refugees
- migrant labor
- oilfield
- ≈ hydroelectric power station

SPAIN

ITALY

TURKEY

GREECE

CYPRUS

SYRIA

LEBANON

ISRAEL

IRAQ

JORDAN

OMAN

YEMEN

Ceuta to Spain
Oran
Algiers
Annaba (Bone)
Tunis
Melilla to Spain
Sétif
Sousse
Malta
Crete

Mediterranean Sea

MOROCCO independent

TUNISIA 1956 independent
Gades
1958
Tripoli
Misurata
Sirte
Benghazi
Derna
Tobruk

ALGERIA
1962 independent
✳1954–62
✳1992
✳1962

LIBYA
1947–51 under Anglo-French administration, 1951 independent

EGYPT
✳1974

Alexandria
Port Said
1956
Cairo
Suez

HOGGAR MASSIF

SAHARA DESERT

TIBESTI MASSIF

MALI independent
1971–74, 1983
(French West Africa)
Gao

NIGER
1960 independent
Agadez
✳1971–74

CHAD
1960 independent
✳from 1968
✳1971–74, 1983, 2004–05

Port Sudan

Red Sea

ERITREA
1941–52 under British administration, 1952–91 to Ethiopia, 1993 independent
✳2001
Massawa
Asmara
✳1970–93
✳1998–2000

Socotra to Yemen

BURKINA FASO independent
1971–75, 1977
Ouagadougou
Niamey
Tahoua
Zinder
Kano

Omdurman
Khartoum
Wad Medani
El Obeid

Mekele
Dese
DJIBOUTI
(French Somaliland)
1977 independent
1983
Djibouti
Berbera
(British Somaliland)
1960 to Somalia

Lake Chad

Darfur
✳from 2003

SUDAN
1956 independent
✳1973, 1998, since 2004

Harer
Somaliland

BENIN
1960 independent
Lake Chad
N'Djamena
Bongor

NIGERIA
1960 independent
✳1967–69
✳1967–70, 1971–74

Sarh
Doba

CENTRAL AFRICAN REPUBLIC
1960 independent
✳1974
Bambari
Bossangoa

South Sudan
✳1958–72, 1981–2003

Addis Ababa
ETHIOPIA
1936–41 to Italy, 1941 independence restored
✳from 1962
1973–79, 1980s–90s, 2001

OGADEN

SOMALIA
1960 independent
✳from 1963
✳1974–75, 1980s–90s, 2000–01
(Italian Somaliland) 1960 to Somalia
Mogadishu
Marka

GHANA independent
1971–74, 1977, 1983
TOGO
1960 independent
Lome
Ilorin
Oshogbo
Abuja
Benue

Accra
Porto Novo
Lagos
Port Harcourt
Yaoundé

Bangui
Ubangi

UGANDA
1962 independent
1980

KENYA
(British East Africa)
1963 independent
✳Mau Mau, 1952–60

Kismaayo

INDIAN OCEAN

CAMEROON
1960 independent
Douala
Bioko (Fernando Póo) to Equatorial Guinea

Kisangani

Lake Turkana
Kampala
Entebbe
Mbale
Kisuma
Meru
Nairobi

Malindi

Victoria
SEYCHELLES
1976 independent

EQUATORIAL GUINEA
(Spanish Guinea)
1968 independent
Bata
Libreville

SÃO TOMÉ & PRÍNCIPE
1975 independent
São Tomé
Port Gentil

GABON
1960 independent

CONGO
1960 independent
✳1960–61

DEMOCRATIC REPUBLIC OF CONGO
(Belgian Congo)
1960 independent, Congo until 1971, Zaire 1971–97
✳1960–65, 1978–97, 1998–2003
✳2001

Congo

RWANDA
1962 independent
✳1962–65, 1995–96
Kigali

BURUNDI
1962 independent
Bujumbura
✳1962–65
✳1972, 1995

TANZANIA
(Tanganyika)
1961 independent, Republic of Tanganyika and Zanzibar until 1964
Dodoma

Lake Victoria
✳1978–79
Mwanza

Tanga
Pemba
Mombasa
Zanzibar
Zanzibar 1963 to Tanzania
Dar es Salaam

Moanda
Brazzaville
Kinshasa
(Leopoldville)
Boma
Port Noire
Cabinda to Angola

Kananga
Mbuji Mayi
Kasai

Kananga

Lake Tanganyika
Katanga

Lake Malawi
✳1983
Mbeya

ATLANTIC OCEAN

Luanda
Malange

ANGOLA
1975 independent
✳1961–75
✳1975–92
✳1971–74, 1983

Benguela
Lobito
Huambo

Namibe
Lubango

Lubumbashi
Mufulira
Chingola
Luanshya
Ndola
Kabwe

ZAMBIA
(Northern Rhodesia)
1964 independent
✳1979, 1983
Lusaka
Livingstone

Kwanza

Cuando

Okavango

MALAWI
(Nyasaland)
1964 independent
2002, 2004
Lilongwe
Nampula
Nacala
Mozambique

Moroni
COMOROS
1975 independent

Mayotte to France

MADAGASCAR
1960 independent
✳1971
Mahajanga
Toamasina
Antananarivo
(Tananarive)

MAURITIUS
1968 independent

Réunion to France

NAMIBIA
(South-West Africa)
1949 to South Africa, 1990 independent
✳1966–90

Swakopmund
Walvis Bay to South Africa until 1994
Windhoek

Keetmanshoop

BOTSWANA
(Bechuanaland)
1966 independent
Francistown
Serowe
Mahalapye
Gaborone

ZIMBABWE
(Southern Rhodesia)
1980 fully independent
✳1966–80 since 2002
Harare (Salisbury)
Mutare
Beira
✳1964–75
✳1971–74, 1983, 2000

MOZAMBIQUE
1975 independent
Quelimane

Madagascar

Toliara

Limpopo

✳1964–94
✳1983
Pretoria
Springs
Johannesburg
Lobamba
Mbabane
Maputo

SWAZILAND
1968 independent
✳1983, 2004

Bloemfontein

Orange
Vaal

Maseru
Durban
LESOTHO
1966 independent
✳1974, 1983, 2004

SOUTH AFRICA
1961 Republic

East London

Cape of Good Hope
Cape Town
Port Elizabeth

Decolonization and Nationalism in Africa

Africans played an active part in World War II, meeting Europeans quite different from the traditional colonial administrators and discovering that the imperial powers were not invincible. They also identified with the democratic freedom for which the Allies were fighting and began to seek their own.

In British West Africa, the white population was small, so the transfer of power was relatively peaceful. The Gold Coast became independent as Ghana and Britain gave independence equally readily to Nigeria, Sierra Leone, and the Gambia by 1965. In Kenya, east Africa, the Mau Mau movement murdered 20,000 people, mostly Kikuyu sympathetic to their white farm-owning masters. Before independence was granted, with Mau Mau leader Jomo Kenyatta as prime minister, British forces were sent in. In contrast, independence movements in Uganda, Tanganyika, Nyasaland, and Northern Rhodesia were relatively peaceful.

Overseas territory

Territory that does not possess full political independence; Africans in French overseas territories were made citizens of the French republic itself.

Former French colonies

French West Africa colonies were replaced by overseas territories. While many Africans accepted this, in order to keep economic links with France, Algeria fought for independence. In 1958 nationalist freedom fighters

End of the Belgian and Portuguese empires

Belgium made no attempt to prepare the Congo for changes in government, and on independence in 1960 the Congolese army mutinied and thousands of Belgian citizens became refugees. Belgian paratroopers went to their aid, and the copper-rich province of Katanga declared its own independence. Eventually, Congolese general Mobutu crushed the Katangans and their mercenary supporters, creating a unified state which he renamed Zaire. Portugal was the last colonial power to leave Africa, and bitterly opposed the nationalists in Guinea, Angola, and Mozambique. By 1975, though, when Portugal underwent its own political convulsions, the colonies became sovereign states.

were confronted by settlers, causing a crisis that brought Charles de Gaulle back to the French presidency. He abandoned the policy of direct rule from Paris, and by 1960 most French colonies had been given independence. De Gaulle abandoned French rule in Algeria in 1962, after losing 10,000 French troops.

Civil war, dictatorship, and corruption

Independence brought few African states stability or prosperity. Many faced ethnic conflict and a legacy of colonial borders; most had poorly educated, impoverished, and rapidly growing populations, and their economies proved vulnerable to multinational companies offering desperately needed investment to exploit the region's natural resources. The experience of Nigeria was typical: a civil war in the late 1960s brought on by a secessionist Igbo revolt led to famine and resulted in a cycle of weak civilian governments replaced by military strong men. Marxist forces, some supported by the Soviet Union or Cuba, fought in many countries, such as Mozambique and Angola, and won control of Ethiopia in 1974. Elsewhere, dictators such as Jean-Bédel Bokassa in the Central African Republic and Uganda's Idi Amin ruled by terror.

A troubled continent

Environmental degradation, as the Sahara spread southward and Africa faced shortages of wood and water, was matched by a demographic crisis in the 1980s as HIV/AIDS swept through central and east Africa. The Organization of African Unity (OAU) and other regional groups foundered through lack of leadership in the face of overwhelming economic problems. The problems of Rwanda in the 1990s, where old ethnic rivalries overflowed into genocide in 1994, creating a flood of refugees into Zaire—itself suffering from civil war—seemed to sum up the intractable problems of the continent.

Curriculum Context

Students should analyze why some African countries achieved independence through constitutional devolution of power and others as a result of armed revolution.

Curriculum Context

The impacts of population pressure, environmental degradation, and poverty are important to understand the breakdown of state authority in various African countries in the 1980s and 1990s.

Glossary

38th Parallel Line of latitude dividing North and South Korea, first established to separate Soviet and U.S. zones after World War II.

Appeasement Tactic of giving in to the demands of an aggressive nation in an attempt to avoid war.

Asian miracle Change of certain South Asian countries from technologically backward and poor to modern, affluent economies.

Battle of Midway Sea battle fought June 4–6, 1942, near the Midway Islands in the Pacific Ocean; a major U.S. victory over the Japanese.

Bay of Pigs Failed attempt by U.S.-backed Cuban exiles to overthrow Fidel Castro's government at the Bay of Pigs, Cuba, on April 17, 1961.

Bolshevik Member of majority Social Democratic Party ("Reds") in Russia.

Command economies Countries where governments make major decisions about the production and distribution of goods and services.

Condominion Joint sovereignty or ownership of the same region.

Exchange Rate Mechanism System for aligning the exchange rates (how much one currency is worth in terms of the other) of EU currencies against each other, to limit fluctuations in currency exchange.

Free-market economics Economic system in which goods and services are bought and sold without government restrictions.

Good Neighbor Policy Declared intention that the United States would no longer intervene in Latin America to protect private U.S. property interests.

Greater East Asian Co-Prosperity Sphere A self-sufficient economic and political bloc created by Japan to form a Great East Asia under Japanese leadership.

Gulag Network of forced labor camps or prisons in the Soviet Union, especially for political opponents to the Communist party.

High technology Most advanced technology currently available, especially electronics and optics, based on intensive research and development, and specialized manufacture.

Intifada Uprising by Palestinian Arabs in the Gaza Strip and the West Bank against Israel.

Iron curtain Political, military, and ideological barrier dividing the Soviet Union and its Communist allies from the West.

Kamikaze Suicide missions by Japanese pilots who crashed their aircraft into enemy ships.

Liberalized A relaxation of government economic restrictions to allow market forces to regulate the relations between economic agents.

Long March Historic 6,000-mile (9,600-km) journey undertaken by Chinese Communist forces to escape the Guomindang.

McCarthy witchhunts Republican senator Joe McCarthy accused thousands of Americans in the 1950s of being Communist sympathizers; many were arrested or lost their jobs.

Mandate Authorization by the League of Nations for a member nation to administer the affairs of another.

Materiel Equipment and supplies of a military force.

Phoney war Period during a war when enemies are not actively engaged in armed conflict.

Politburo The chief executive and political committee of the Soviet Communist Party.

Revaluation Alteration of the relative value of a currency, based on criteria such as wage rates or the international price of gold, causing a rise in the price of goods or products.

Sanctions Trade limits or other punishments used to ensure compliance, such as 1970s restriction of OPEC oil exports.

Secede To withdraw from membership of a political alliance.

Special economic zone Region with different economic rules from the rest of a country, set up to generate investment, exports, employment, and development of infrastructure.

Tamil Tigers Terrorist organization in Sri Lanka that seeks to establish an independent Tamil state using guerrilla tactics.

Theocratic Government with religious leaders who rule as representatives of their god or deity using a legal system based on religious principles.

Total war The complete mobilization of a country's resources and economy towards its war efforts.

United Arab Republic Arab-Muslim union formed by Egypt and Syria.

Vietminh North Vietnamese organization, led by Ho Chi Minh to drive the French from their Indo-China colony.

Western Front Line of battle between the Allies and Germany in WWI, which stretched from the English Channel across France and Belgium.

Further Research

BOOKS

Aylett, J. F., and Neil DeMarco. *The Cold War and After* (Hodder 20th Century History). Hodder Murray, 2005.

Best, Antony, Hanhimäki, Jussi, Joseph A. Maiolo, and Kirsten E. Schulze. *An International History of the Twentieth Century*. Routledge, 2003.

Bowden, Rob. *Globalization: The Impact on Our Lives* (21st Century Debates). Raintree, 2004.

Chapman, Victoria L., and David Lindroth. *World History on File: The 20th Century*. Facts on File, 2006.

Corey, Melinda. *Chronology of 20th-century America* (Decades of American History). Facts on File, 2006.

DeMarco, Neil. *The Second World War* (Hodder 20th Century History). Hodder & Stoughton, 2004.

Howard, Michael, and William Roger Louis (eds). *The Oxford History of Twentieth Century*. Oxford University Press, 2002.

Maus, Derek. *Turning Points in World History — The Cold War*. Greenhaven Press, 2002.

Roberts, J. M. *Emerging Powers* (The Illustrated History of the World, Volume 9). Oxford University Press, 2002.

Roberts, J. M. *The New Global Era* (The Illustrated History of the World, Volume 10). Oxford University Press, 2002.

Roberts, J. M. *The Penguin History of the Twentieth Century: The History of the World, 1901 to the Present* (Allen Lane History). Penguin, 2004.

Robertshaw, Andrew, and Mark Bergin. *Warfare in the 20th Century: The Age of Global Conflict* (Battle Zones). Peter Bedrick, 2004.

INTERNET RESOURCES

BBC History. This website has a special section on the world wars with pages about World War I and II, Nazi genocide, and the politico-economic situations that led to wars and the Cold War of the later 20th century.
www.bbc.co.uk/history/worldwars/

Channel 4. Highly illustrated British TV station web guide linked to different aspects of the 20th century, including wars and globalization. There is detailed information on some key figures including Fidel Castro, Joseph Stalin, and John F. Kennedy.
www.channel4.com/history/microsites/H/history/browse/1900-2000.html

Did you know? A very useful timeline of 20th century events for each year of the century.
www.didyouknow.org/history/20thcentury.htm

Eyewitness to History. A site that features eyewitness accounts of key historical events. The World War II section has fascinating personal descriptions of significant events, for example key moments in the war in the Pacific such as the Battle of Midway and being on ships during kamikaze attacks.
www.eyewitnesstohistory.com/w1frm.htm

Public Broadcasting Service. A vast selection of websites on different themes, many linked with PBS TV shows, including historical. The Great War pages include primary sources such as interviews with soldiers along with maps and a useful timeline.
www.pbs.org/greatwar/

Spartacus Educational. This history site provides facts, illustrations, and biographies on a wide variety of topics relating to 20th century history, such as Nazi Germany, McCarthyism, and Black Power.
www.spartacus.schoolnet.co.uk

World Bank. The World Bank remains a major international organization promoting globalization. Read their take on the history of global economic cooperation and globalization issues today.
http://youthink.worldbank.org/issues/globalization/

Index

Page numbers in *italic* refer to illustrations.

Afghanistan 57, 82, 83
Africa 10, 12, 24, 28, 102–105
African-Americans 40, 44
agriculture 41, 48, 49, 53, 56, 57, 75, 76, 82
airforces 24, 28
Albania 33
Algeria 104, 105
Allied Powers/ Forces (Allies), 16, 17, 20, 22, 24, 25, 26, 28, 29, 32, 40, 60, 61, 64, 68, 70, 71, 74, 80, 93, 104
appeasement 21
Arab–Israeli Conflict 94–97, 98, 100, 101
Arab League 8, 10
Arafat, Yassir 100, 101
Argentina 41, 45
armed forces 41, 70, 75
    American 32, 61, 65, 68, 69, 75, 76
    British 24, 25, 104
    Bulgarian 25, 28
    Chinese 69, 76
    German 16, 17, 21, 24, 25, 28, 29, 56
    Japanese 58, 65, 68, 69
    Red (Russian or Soviet) 16, 28, 29, 52, 56, 57, 74, 82, 83
Armenia 37
Asian miracle 89
Aswan Dam 96
atomic bomb *see* nuclear weapons
Aung San, General 82
Aung San, Suu Kyi 82
Australia 68, 89
Austria 21
Austria–Hungary 14, 16, 17, 18, 20
Axis forces 25, 29
Azerbaijan 37

Balkans 16, 17,
Baltic states 24, 25, 52, 53, 56, 57
Bangladesh 76, 78, 81
Barbarossa campaign 24, 25
Battle of Britain 24
Battle of the Atlantic 28
Battle of the Coral Sea 68
Battle of Iwo Jima 69, *70*
Battle of Leyte Gulf 69
Battle of the Philippine Sea 69
Begin, Prime Minister Menachem 97, 100
Belgium 16, 24, 28

Belgian empire 104
Belize, 49
Berlin Blockade 32, 33
Bhutto, Benazir 82
Bhutto, Zulfikar Ali 82
Black Power 49
Blitz 24, 25
Bolshevik 17, 52, 53
Bosnia–Herzegovina 37
Brazil 40, 41
Brezhnev, Leonid 57
Britain 6, 14, 17, 20, 21, 24, 25, 36, 40, 41, 49, 53, 60, 61, 64, 96, 104
    British empire 64, 65, 68, 77, 80, 92, 104
Bulgaria 28, 33
Burma 64, 68, 70, 76, 77, 82, 89

Cambodia 76, 89
Camp David 100, 101
Canada 40, 41, 45, 57, 89
Cárdenas, Lázaro 41
Caribbean islands 40, 41, 46–49
Carter, President Jimmy 100
Castro, Fidel 44, 48
Caucasus 25, 52, 57, 83
Central African Republic 105
Central America 38–39, 41, 46–49
Central Asia 78–83
Central Powers 16, 17,
chemical weapons 101
Chiang Kai-shek *see* Jiang Jieshi
Chile 41, 45
China 6, 12, 56, 58–61, 64, 65, 69, 75, 76, 77, 78, 82, 83, 86, 87, 88, 89
    People's Liberation Army (PLA) 61, 75, 76
Chinese Communist Party (CCP) 60, 61, 65, 76
Churchill, Prime Minister Winston 24, 28
civil rights campaigns 44
civil wars 29, 37, 52, 57, 65, 74, 80, 83, 92, 100, 101, 102, 105
Cold War 8, 32, 33, 34, 36, 37, 44, 75, 83
collectivization 53, 76
Colombia 41, 45
colonialism 8, 17, 62, 64, 65, 74, 76, 92, 93, 102, 104, 105
Commonwealth, British 64, 74, 89
Commonwealth of Independent States (CIS) 57
Communist/ism 8, 12, 21, 29, 32, 33, 36, 37, 44, 48, 49, 50, 52, 53, 56, 57, 60, 65, 74, 76, 77, 83, 87, 88, 89
Congo 104

Congress party *see* Indian National Congress
Croatia 37
Cuba 41, 44, 46, 48, 105
    Cuban Missile Crisis/ Bay of Pigs 44, 48, 56
Cultural Revolution 76
Czarist 17, 50
Czechoslovakia 10, 20, 21, 33, 37

Dalai Lama 83
death camps 25, 29
decolonization 102, 103, 104, 105
De Gaulle, President Charles 105
Deng Xiaoping 88
Denmark 24, 36
détente 57
dictatorships 18, 41, 45, 105
Dominican Republic 49
drug trafficking 36, 45, 49
Dutch East Indies 65, 68, 77

East Asia 72, 73, 74, 75, 76, 77
economic depression 21, 40, 64
Ecuador 45
education 44, 49, 76, 88, 105
Egypt 25, 93, 96, 101
El Salvador 48, 49
environmental issues 42, 45
Ethiopia 21, 93, 105
European Community (EC) 33, 36
European Union 36
Exchange Rate Mechanism (ERM) 36

Fascism 21, 53, 93
Falkland Islands 45
Finland 24
food exports/ imports 28, 41, 56, 74
France 6, 14, 16, 20, 21, 24, 28, 33, 53, 60, 64, 65, 92, 93, 96
    French empire 76, 92, 93, 104
Franco, General 21
French Indo-China 61, 65, 76, 77
fundamentalism 77, 82, 83, 100

Gandhi, Indira *81*
Gandhi, Mohandas 64, 80
Gandhi, Rajiv 82
Gaza 96, 100, 101
genocide 105
Germany 14, 16, 17, 20, 21, 24, 28, 29, 60, 71
    East (German Democratic Republic) 32, 33, 36
    Reunification 36
    West 32, 33, 36
German empire 20, 92

glasnost 57
"Good Neighbor" Policy 41
Gorbachev, Mikhail 33, 57
Great Depression 40, 64
Great Leap Forward 75, 76
Greece 25, 28, 29
Grenada 49
Guantanamo Bay 41, 48
Guatemala 48, 49
guerrillas 29, 49, 61, 76, 77, 80, 83
gulag 53
Gulf War 101
Guomindang (KMT—Nationalist
    Party) 60, 61

Haiti 49
Halsey, Admiral William 69
healthcare 44, 45
Helsinki Agreement 33
high technology 84, 86, 87
Hirohito, Emperor 71, 74
Hitler, Adolf 21, 22, 24, 25, 26, 28,
    29, 53, 65
Ho Chi Minh 76
Holocaust 29, 92
Honduras 48
Hong Kong 68, 86, 87, 88, 89
human rights 48, 88
Hungary 10, 28, 33
Hussein, President Saddam 100,
    101

imperialism 16, 21, 61, 64, 65
India 64, 64, 68, 78, 80, 81, 82, 83
Indian National Congress 64, 80,
    81
Indonesia 77, 88
industrialization 16, 44, 45, 53,
    75, 76, 82, 84, 87, 88
industrial disputes 33, 40, 45, 49,
    65
industries 44, 48, 53, 81, 86, 88,
    93
    heavy 40, 41, 56, 87, 88
    space 44, 56, 82
inflation 20, 33, 37, 45, 61
infrastructure 41, 86, 87, 88, 89
Intifada 101
Iran 83, 98, 100, 101
Iran–Iraq War 100
Iraq 92, 96, 97, 98, 100, 101
Iron Curtain 32
isolationism 6, 21
Israel 92, 94–97, 98, 100, 101
Italy 20, 21, 24, 25, 28, 93

Japan 6, 60, 61, 62–65, 66, 68, 69,
    71, 74, 86, 87, 88
Jerusalem 96
Jew(ish) 25, 29, 92, 96, 101

Jiang Ching-kuo 87
Jiang Jieshi (Chiang Kai-shek) 60,
    61, 76, 87
Jinnah, Mohammed 80
Jordan 96, 97

kamikaze 69
Kennedy, President John F. 48
Kenya 104
Kenyatta, Prime minister Jomo
    104
Kim Il Sung 74, 87
Korea 64, 71, 74, 75, 87
Korean War 32, 33, 75
Khomeini, Ayatollah 100
Khrushchev, Nikita 48, 56, 57
Kuwait 98, 101

labor 33, 40, 41, 86, 87, 88, 89
Laos 76, 89
Latin America 38–39, 41, 42–45
League of Nations 6, 20, 40, 64,
    92
Lebanon 92, 97, 100
Lenin, Vladimir Ilyich 52
Libya 93, 97
Long March 60

MacArthur, Douglas 69, 74
Malaya 68, 77
Malaysia 86, 88
Manchu dynasty 58, 60, 64
Manchuria 61, 64, 71
Marshall Aid 32
Marxism/ist 20, 45, 49, 60, 75, 105
McCarthy, Senator Joseph 44
Menem, Carlos 45
Mexico 41, 49
Middle East 16, 90–93, 98–101
migration 36, 49, 80, 89, 92, 94
military technology 16, 17, 25,
    28, 29, 40, 56, 57, 71, 82
Mountbatten, Lord Louis 69, 80
Mozambique 104, 105
Mubarak, President Hosni 100
Mujibur, Sheikh 81
Mujihadeen 83
Munich Agreement 21
munitions 16, 17, 25, 28, 33, 40,
    101
Muslim League 80
Mussolini, Benito 21, 28, 93

Najibullah, President 83
Nasser, Colonel Gamal 96
nation–state 20
nationalisation 41, 82
nationalism 20, 37, 44, 56, 60, 61,
    64, 65, 69, 76, 77, 80, 82, 87,
    90, 93, 96, 102, 104

NATO (North Atlantic Treaty
    Organisation) 8, 32, 36, 37, 56
North Korea 12
Nazi 21, 25, 28, 29, 71, 92
Nazi–Soviet Pact 24, 53
Nehru, Jawaharlal 64, 80
Netherlands 24, 64
New Deal 41
New Zealand 89
Nicaragua 48, 49
Nigeria 104, 105
Nimitz, Admiral Chester 69
Noriega, Manuel 49
North Africa 24, 28, 90–93
North American Free Trade
    Agreement 45
North Korea 74, 75, 87, 89
Norway 24
nuclear weapons 33, 44, 48, 56,
    66, 71, 82

Obama, President Barack 101
oil 10, 33, 41, 49, 65, 68, 90, 92,
    93, 97, 98, 100, 101
OPEC (Organization of Petroleum
    Exporting Countries) 10, 45, 97
Ortega, Daniel 49
Ottoman empire 16, 17, 20, 92

Pacific Rim 84–89
Pakistan 76, 78, 80, 81, 82
Palestine 92, 94–97, 98, 101
Palestinian Liberation
    Organization (PLO) 97, 100
Panama 49
    Canal 41
Partition (India) 80
Pearl Harbor 65, 68, 69
Perestroika 57
Peróns 45
Peru 45
Philippines 64, 68, 70, 76, 88
phoney war 24
Poland 20, 21, 24, 25, 29, 33, 52,
    53, 56
Portuguese empire 64, 104
poverty 29, 44, 60, 81, 86

Rabin, Prime Minister Yitzhak 101
Reagan, President Ronald 57
refugees 32, 80, 82, 94, 97, 104
reparations 20
revolt/revolution 12, 20, 33, 45,
    46, 47, 48, 50, 52, 53, 60, 77
Romania 17, 28, 33
Roosevelt, President Franklin 28,
    41
rubber 65, 68
Russia 12, 14, 16, 17, 18, 20, 37,
    50, 53

Russian Federation 57
Russo-Japanese War 64
Rwanda 105

Sadat, President Anwar 97, 100
sanctions 48, 61, 97, 101
Sandinista 49
Saudi Arabia 97, 101
Selassie, Haile 93
Serbia, 17
Siberia 52
Sinai 96, 100, 101
Singapore 86, 87, 88, 89
Sino-Soviet Treaty 75
Six-Day War 96
Slovakia 29
socialism 44, 52, 75, 82
Soviet Union 10, 12, 21, 24, 25,
    28, 29, 30, 32, 33, 34, 36, 37,
    41, 44, 48, 49, 50–57, 60, 61,
    71, 74, 82, 83, 96, 101, 105
South America 38, 39, 41, 42, 43,
    45
South Asia 78–83
South Korea 74, 75, 86, 87
southeast Asia 10, 66, 68, 69, 81
Spanish Civil War 21
Sri Lanka 82, 83
Stalin, Joseph 25, 29, 52, 53, 56,
    71
Stalingrad 28
strikes see industrial disputes
Sudan 93
Suez Canal 93, 96
Sun Yixian (Sun Yat-sen) 60
Syria 92, 93, 96, 97, 100, 101

Taiwan 61, 76, 86, 87, 88
Tamil Tigers 83
terrorism 33, 36, 83, 97, 100
Thailand 77, 88
Thatcher, Prime Minister
    Margaret 33
Tibet 75, 78, 83
tiger economies 86, 88
Tito, Josip 29
Tojo, Hideki 68
Treaty of Versailles 20, 21, 40
Trinidad and Tobago 49
Truman, President Harry S. 71
Turkey 101

Uganda 104, 105
Ukraine 17, 52, 56
unemployment 21, 33, 37, 45, 49
United Arab Republic 96
United Kingdom 16
United Nations 8, 37, 61, 74, 75,
    80, 92, 96, 101

United States 6, 17, 20, 25, 28, 30,
    31, 32, 33, 37, 38–45, 48, 49,
    57, 65, 66, 68, 74, 75, 76, 77,
    86, 87, 88, 89, 96, 97, 100, 101
USSR see Soviet Union

V-bomb 29
Venezuela 41, 45
Vichy 24
Vietnam, 12, 64, 76, 87, 89
Vietnam War 33, 87

Warsaw Pact 10, 32, 36
weapons see munitions
West Africa 104
Western Front 16, 17
Wilhelm II, Kaiser 17
Wilson, President Woodrow 20,
    40
World War I 6, 14–17, 20, 21, 24,
    40, 52, 64, 92, 93
World War II 8, 21, 22–29, 30, 32,
    41, 42, 44, 53, 54, 56, 61, 65,
    66–71, 72, 74, 76, 80, 82, 87,
    92, 93, 102, 104

Yamamoto, Isoroko 68
Yeltsin, Boris 37, 57
Yom Kippur War 97
Yuan Shikai 60
Yugoslavia 20, 25, 29, 33, 37
    war in Yugoslavia 37

Zapatista 49
Zedong, Mao 60, 61, 75, 76, 77,
    88
Zia ul-Haq, President 72